Pastoral Prayers

Pastoral Prayers

A Resource for Pastoral Occasions

EDITED BY
Richard Deadman
Jeremy Fletcher
Janet Hudson
Stephen Oliver

BLOOMSBURY CONTINUUM
LONDON • OXFORD • NEW YORK • NEW DELHI • SYDNEY

BLOOMSBURY CONTINUUM
Bloomsbury Publishing Plc
50 Bedford Square, London, WC1B 3DP, UK
29 Earlsfort Terrace, Dublin 2, Ireland

BLOOMSBURY, BLOOMSBURY CONTINUUM and the Diana logo are
trademarks of Bloomsbury Publishing Plc

First published 1996
© in the arrangement: the editors 1996
Cover illustration: Regina M. Rynja OSB

For further copyright information on individual items, see Sources and
Acknowledgements on pp. 127–9. Numbers in the right-hand margin
refer to this list.

A catalogue record for this book is available from the British Library

Library of Congress Cataloguing-in-Publication data has been applied for

ISBN: HB: 9781472968487

6 8 10 9 7 5

Printed and bound in Great Britain by CPI Group (UK) Ltd, Croydon CR0 4YY

MIX
Paper | Supporting
responsible forestry
FSC® C013604

To find out more about our authors and books visit www.bloomsbury.com and
sign up for our newsletters

Contents

Foreword

There are many occasions in pastoral ministry when it is helpful to have prayers and short readings to hand, collected and arranged so that they can be found easily.

For many years, clergy have valued a priest's 'Vade Mecum' that they carry in their pockets; in addition a number of further pastoral needs and opportunities have been identified, but there has been no comparable publication since the substantial work of liturgical revision began to be undertaken.

This book seeks to serve this need, and will be an invaluable resource to all those engaged in pastoral work – the readers and lay pastoral assistants as much as the ordained clergy – and I commend it warmly.

David Stancliffe
Bishop of Salisbury
April 1996

Preface

Pastoral ministry is intensely personal. It involves both sharing the delights of joyful celebration and bearing times of unimaginable pain and anguish. No one can meet the demands of this soul-searching ministry but by the grace of God in Christ. Above all it is a ministry of prayer. The willingness and confidence to pray with integrity are what make this ministry so valued and unique.

Yet it is impossible to make provision for every pastoral situation. In practice there is always the essential prerequisite to remain open to the Spirit of God if the needs of the moment are to be discerned with sensitive insight.

This collection of prayers and readings is intended to be a flexible resource rather than a rigid manual. A judicious use of words with silence and stillness in the presence of God may well be more appropriate in the circumstances.

It is our prayer that this anthology will prove to be a helpful encouragement to those who enjoy the enormous privilege of sharing the ministry of Christ today.

Stephen Oliver
Editor
Leeds 1996

Personal prayers for those in pastoral ministry

Fulfil the ministry which you have received in the Lord.
COLOSSIANS 4.17

Pastoral ministry is to share in the ministry of Christ. Prayer is the essential prerequisite if that authentic ministry is to be exercised with perception, patience and perseverance. The ministry of Christ begins, continues and ends in prayer.

Preparatory prayers

Lord Jesus Christ, you know well my strength and weakness.
I come to you in faith to be used in your service.

Let me work within my competence
not reach beyond my ability.

Sustain me in your service.

Let me be confident in your saving power
not arrogant in my self-esteem.

Teach me in your service.

Let me learn from your life
not lean on my strength alone.

Protect me in your service.

Let me be open to your Word
not distracted in my listening.

Into your hands I commend my spirit.
Keep me in your service now and forever.   (19)

God of truth,
make me sensitive
to suffering that is unseen;
to hurt that masquerades as hate
and fear that fuels anger;
to frustration that flows in tears
and laughter which hides the pain.
Let me not be hasty in judgement
but perceptive in understanding
for Jesus Christ's sake.   (19)

Spirit of God,
make me open to others in listening,
generous to others in giving,
and sensitive to others in praying
through Jesus Christ.   (22)

Lord Jesus Christ,
you ate and drank
with the powerful and the poor;
you called the sick to your side
and sinners into your company.
In the manner of your ministry
let me be of service today,
neither fearing the strong
nor favouring the rich.
Strengthen me with ample power
to meet whatever comes

with fortitude, patience and joy,
and in all things to give you thanks and praise.   (19)

In conflict and crisis

Merciful God,
give me the courage
to face this moment,
and save me from the cowardice
which tempts me to turn away.   (19)

Pastoral crisis

God of all care and compassion
you take us through deep waters
but never abandon us in the storm;
we walk in the dark
but you never leave us without light.
Be with us in the night of our anxiety
and in the day of our over-confidence
that we may keep faith with each other
as you have kept faith with us in
Jesus Christ our Lord.   **Amen.**   (19)

Laying down the load

Come to me all who labour and are heavy laden,
and I will give you rest.
I am gentle and lowly of heart,
and you will find rest for your souls.
For my yoke is easy and my burden is light.

Matthew 11.28–30

Gentle and gracious God,
accept all that I bring to you,
the words I have heard;
the suffering I have seen;
the joy I have shared;
the people I have met;
and the lessons I have learned
of your mercy, truth and love
in Jesus Christ, my Lord and my God.   (19)

Into your hands I commend my spirit,
for you have redeemed me, Lord God of truth.

Keeping a confidence

Holy Spirit
inspire the words on my lips
and guard my tongue from speaking evil;
keep me from careless talk
that nothing I say
may betray the trust placed in me.   (19)

House and home

The blessing of a home

The prayers which follow are particularly for new occupation of a home. Where the request to bless a home comes because of distressing circumstances or evil attack, prayers in the 'Deliverance' section will also be appropriate. A prayer for the blessing of salt and water will be found there.

Introduction

MINISTER   Peace be to this house.
ALL   And to all who dwell in it.

Lord God, holy, blessed and glorious Trinity bless, hallow and sanctify this house that in it there may be joy and gladness, peace and love, health and goodness, and thanksgiving always to you, Father Son and Holy Spirit; and let your blessing rest upon this house and those who dwell in it, now and for ever. **Amen.**

To God alone be the glory for ever and ever. **Amen.**

For the occupants

> May Christ always be here with you.
> May he share in your joys,
> and comfort you in your sorrows.
> May he inspire and help you
> to make your home
> a dwelling place of love,
> offering the kindly hospitality of God. **Amen**.   (21)

For protection

> Father, Son and Holy Spirit,
> one God, blessed for ever:
> expel and put away from this house
> all power and presence of darkness.
> Watch over and defend this home,
> and let no evil come near your servants,
> that they may be guarded by your angels
> and folded in your eternal love. **Amen.**   (21)

Prayers for individual places in the home

At the door

> May the door of this home be wide enough
> to receive all who need human love and friendship.
> May it welcome all who have cares to unburden,
> thanks to express, hopes to nurture.
> May the door of this house/place be narrow enough
> to shut out pettiness and pride, envy and enmity.
> May its threshold be no stumbling block
> to young or strained feet.

May it be too high to admit complacency,
selfishness and harshness.
May this home be for all who enter,
the doorway to your eternal kingdom.   **Amen.**   (11)

In a bedroom

Lord God our heavenly Father, you neither slumber nor
sleep. Bless the bedrooms of this house and guard with
your continual watchfulness all who take rest within
these walls, that refreshed by the gift of sleep they may
wake to serve you joyfully in their daily work; through
Jesus Christ our Lord.   **Amen.**

In a child's room

Almighty God our heavenly Father, your blessed Son at
Nazareth shared the life of an earthly home. Bless all children who shall live in this house and grant wisdom and
understanding to all who have care for them, that they
may grow up in your constant fear and love; through
Jesus Christ our Lord.   **Amen.**

In the kitchen

Grant, Lord, to all who shall work in this room that in
serving others they may serve you and share in your perfect service, and that in the busyness of the kitchen they
may possess you in tranquillity; through Jesus Christ our
Lord.   **Amen.**

At the dining table

> Lord God, you give good things liberally and without stint. Grant that all who shall eat and drink together at this table may be joined in true friendship and may praise you with thankful hearts; through Jesus Christ our Lord. **Amen.**

In the study

> Lord, you are the true Light that lightens everyone who comes into the world. Bless this place of study, that those who work here may come to the knowledge of your will, and daily increase in spiritual understanding of the love and glory of the one true God who lives and reigns, Father, Son and Holy Spirit, world without end. **Amen.**

In the living room

> Lord God, your blessed Son has said, 'Henceforth I have called you friends.' Unite in true friendship and love all who shall meet in this room; through Jesus Christ our Lord.   (23)

A final prayer

> Hear God's word of benediction:
> the fruit of righteousness will be peace
> and the result of righteousness
> tranquillity and trust for ever.
> My people will abide
> in secure dwellings
> and in quiet resting places.

And now the eternal Spirit,
enfold this home with love;
indwell this home with joy;
and build this home in peace
evermore and evermore.   **Amen.**   (5)

The ministry of deliverance

Preface: a health warning

There will be times in pastoral ministry when a situation arises
where bondage to, or oppression by, an evil influence requires
prayer (see Mark 9.29). The ministry of deliverance is complex and
can be difficult, requiring sensitivity and experience. Each denom-
ination, and every diocese in the Church of England, has specialist
advisers available. No ministry should be undertaken unless
proper preparation has been made and professional advice has
been sought. It is always necessary to have prayer support.

These prayers are offered as a framework, and for those who
feel a need to pray something, perhaps as a general preparation for
further specialist help. You are strongly advised to read further in
this area: M. Perry (ed.), *Deliverance* (SPCK, 1987) and John
Richards, *Exorcism, Deliverance and Healing* (Grove Worship
Series no. 44; Grove Books, 1976) both contain liturgical material.

Wherever practicable, there should always be an act of confession and absolution, a renunciation of occult or other evil involve-
ment, and a declaration of the Lordship of Christ.

Personal preparation

St Patrick's breastplate

> Christ be with me, Christ within me,
> Christ behind me, Christ before me,
> Christ beside me, Christ to win me,
> Christ to comfort and restore me.
> Christ beneath me, Christ above me,
> Christ in quiet, Christ in danger,
> Christ in hearts of all that love me,
> Christ in mouth of friend and stranger.
>
> I bind unto myself the Name,
> The strong Name of the Trinity;
> By invocation of the same,
> The Three in One and One in Three.
> Of whom all nature hath creation;
> Eternal Father, Spirit, Word:
> Praise to the Lord of my salvation,
> Salvation is of Christ the Lord.
>
> Jesus,
> May all that is you flow into me;
> May your Body and your Blood be my food and drink;
> May your passion and death be my strength and my life;
> May the shelter I seek be the shadow of your cross;
> Let me not run from the love which you offer,
> But hold me safe from the forces of evil.
> On each of my dyings shed your light and your love.
> Keep calling me until that day comes
> when with your saints I may praise you forever.   (28)

The shield of the Father
Covering, caring
From evil's snaring
The shield of the Son
New life supplying
Defence against dying.
The shield of the Spirit
A shelter discover
Where we can recover.
The shield of the Three
For body and soul
The shield of the Three
Keeping us whole.   (25)

An introductory prayer

Lord, you gave to your church authority to act in your
Name. We ask you therefore to visit today what we visit,
and to bless whatever we bless; and grant that as we enter
this house in lowliness of heart, all powers of evil may be
put to flight and the angel of peace may enter in. Defend
from harm all who enter and leave this door, and give
your protection to the members of this household in their
going out and their coming in; through Jesus Christ our
Lord. **Amen.**   (23)

For deliverance

Heavenly and loving Father,
we come to you in the name of King Jesus,
and in virtue of his blood shed for us.
We declare our absolute dependence on you,
for apart from Christ we can do nothing.

All authority in heaven and earth
has been given to him,
and in his name we claim that authority
over all spiritual enemies and power,
especially the evil one troubling *N*.

In the name of Christ we bind that evil spirit
and command it to depart to the place reserved for it
never to affect *N* again.
Fill *N* with your Holy Spirit,
and bring him/her to the glorious freedom
of your sons and daughters.   (35)

From all evil and mischief;
from sin, and from the crafts and assaults of the devil:
Good Lord, deliver us/*N*/me.

In the name of Jesus of Nazareth, Son of the Most
   High God,
I bind you, evil spirit(s)
and command you to leave this person,
to harm no one,
and to go to your own place, never to return.   **Amen.**

Lord God of Hosts, before your presence the armies of
hell are put to flight. Deliver *N* from the assaults and
temptations of the evil one. Free him/her from every evil
and unclean spirit that may be assailing him/her.
Strengthen and protect him/her by the power of your
Holy Spirit; through Jesus Christ our Lord.   **Amen.**

Be gone, Satan, and cease to trouble this servant of God.
In the Name of Jesus Christ.   **Amen.**   (28)

A prayer of blessing for salt and water for use in a house

Blessed are you, Lord, God of all creation; through your goodness we have this salt and water to be hallowed by the invocation of your holy Name. As salt was made by the Lord's word to be the symbol of his disciples in the world, and as water was consecrated for the rebirth of his people in baptism, so we mix this salt and water in the Name of the Father and of the Son and of the Holy Spirit; and we pray that wherever it is sprinkled, all evil may be banished and your blessing may abide there; through Jesus Christ our Lord.   **Amen.**   (23)

Prayer for a place

Visit, Lord, we pray, this place, and drive from it all the snares of the enemy. Let your holy angels dwell here to keep us in peace, and may your blessing be upon it evermore; through Jesus Christ our Lord.   **Amen.**

A prayer of expulsion

Be gone from this place, every evil haunting and
   phantasm;
Depart for ever, every unclean spirit;
Be banished, every delusion and deceit of Satan;
Be put to flight, every evil power.
In the name of the living God.
In the name of the holy God.
In the name of the God of all creation.
In the name of Jesus Christ his only Son, and in the
   Power of his Holy Spirit.   **Amen.**   (23)

In the Name of God, Father, Son and Holy Spirit: we order you, every evil spirit, to leave this place, harming no one, and to go to the place appointed you.   **Amen.**   (23)

We praise you, Lord, that you have delivered your servant *N* from these wicked spirits. Come to him/her, Lord, with the goodness and peace of your Son Jesus Christ, that he/she may have no fear, nor be troubled any more by the power of evil. We ask this through your Son Jesus Christ, our Saviour and Redeemer.   **Amen.**   (28)

May our Lord Jesus Christ himself, and God our Father, who loved us and in his grace has given us unfailing courage and a firm hope, encourage and comfort you, that you may always do and say what is good. May the Lord who is faithful strengthen you, and keep you safe from the evil one. And now may the Lord of peace himself give you peace at all times and in every way.

2 Thessalonians 2.16–17; 3.3, 16

And the blessing of God Almighty, the Father, the Son and the Holy Spirit, be among you and remain with you always.   **Amen.**   (28)

Almighty God, heavenly Father,
breathe your Holy Spirit into the heart of this your
    servant *N*
inspire him/her with love for goodness and truth;
May he/she, fearing only to be faithless, have no other
    fear;
May he/she, knowing your Fatherhood, be ever mindful
    of your love;
May he/she, in serving you faithfully until death, live
    eternally with you;
through Jesus Christ our Lord.   **Amen.**   (28)

A blessing

May the risen and ascended Christ, mightier than the hordes of hell, more glorious than the heavenly hosts, be with you in all your ways.   **Amen.**

May his cross protect you by day and by night, at all times and in all places.   **Amen.**

May he guard and deliver you from the snares of the devil, from the assaults of evil spirits, from the wrath of the wicked, from all base passions and from the fear of the known and unknown.   **Amen.**

May the saints of God pray for you, and the angels of God guard and protect you.   **Amen.**

And may the Lord of heaven and earth grant you freedom from your sins, and all the riches of his grace. **Amen.**

The blessing of God almighty, the Father, the Son and the Holy Spirit, be upon you and remain with you always. **Amen.**   (28)

3

New life

The blessing of a pregnant woman

O Lord and giver of life, receive our prayer for *N* and for the child she has conceived, that they may happily come to the time of birth, and serving you in all things may rejoice in your loving providence. We ask this through our Lord Jesus Christ, who lives and reigns with you and the Holy Spirit, one God, now and for ever. **Amen.**

(Any or all of the following may be added.)

Blessed are you, Lord God, you have blessed the union of *N* and *N*. **Amen.**

Blessed are you, Lord God. May your blessing be upon *N* and the child she carries. **Amen.**

Blessed are you, Lord God. May this time of pregnancy be for *N* and *N* months of drawing nearer to you and to one another. **Amen.**

Blessed are you, Lord God. May *N* and *N*'s experience of birth be full of awe and wonder and joy at sharing in your creation. **Amen.**

Blessed are you, Lord God. Let the fullness of your blessings be upon those whom we bless in your name: Father, Son and Holy Spirit.　**Amen.**　　　　　　(37)

Prayers before the birth

Loving God, we thank you for your gracious invitation to share in the gift of creation.

Bless *N* as she approaches the time for the delivery of her baby/babies.

In your compassion, give her strength to endure the pain she will feel in the bringing forth of a new life.

Protect both her and her child/children from harm and grant them a safe passage through the exertions of labour.

Grant that soon they may rest together, rejoicing in one another and in your love for them through Jesus Christ, our Lord.　**Amen.**　　　　　　(18)

Creator God, as you were with Sarah and Hannah and Mary at the births of their children, so be continually with *N*, helping her to have a sure confidence in you as she awaits the birth of the child you have given her.　**Amen.** (18)

Prayer with a father-to-be

Lord Jesus Christ, who shared the pains of a human life, wait with us as we wait with *N* (*mother's name*). Bring her relief during her labour and grant that *N* (*father's name*) may soon know that the pains of birth have not been in vain as he and *N* (*mother's name*) share the joy of seeing their child.　**Amen.**　　　　　　(18)

Prayer for parents facing an uncertain outcome to labour

God of the present moment,
God who in Jesus stills the storm
and soothes the frantic heart,
bring hope and courage to *N* (and *N*)
as he/she/they wait(s) in uncertainty.
Bring hope that will make him/her/them the equal
of whatever lies ahead.
Bring him/her/them courage to endure what cannot be
avoided,
for your will is health and wholeness;
you are God and we need you.   **Amen.**   (5)

Thanksgiving

For a mother after the delivery of her child

Holy Spirit of God, creator and sustainer of human life,
we praise you that you have called *N*
to share in your creative acts by the great mystery of
childbirth.
We give you thanks that she has been brought safely
through the time of pregnancy and labour,
bringing new life into this world which you love,
in the name of Him who was born of a woman,
Jesus Christ, our Redeemer.   **Amen.**   (5)

The blessing of the God of Sarah and of Abraham,
The blessing of the Son, born of Mary,
The blessing of the Spirit, who broods over us
as a mother over her children,
be with you now and for ever.   **Amen.**   (5)

Short thanksgiving for the birth of a child

> Creator God, you made the universe yet you number
>   the very hairs of our head.
> We praise you for the miracle of the birth of *N*'s child
>   (*N, if name is chosen*);
> thank you for bringing them safely through the
>   experience of birth;
> in the pain and the relief,
> in the tears and the joy,
> in the support of family (friends) and midwives,
> in the gift of new life and in parenthood,
> may they continue to know the power of your creating
>   and caring love,
> through Jesus Christ our Lord.   **Amen.**   (18)

Adapted Psalms for use before and after birth

God is my strong rock in whom I trust

> God is my strong rock in whom I trust,
> and all my confidence I rest in her.
>
> Deep in my mother's womb, she knew me;
> before my limbs were formed, she yearned for me.
> Each of my movements she remembers with
>   compassion,
> and when I was still unseen, she did imagine me.
>
> Her strength brought me forth into the light;
> it was she who delivered me.
> Hers were the hands that held me safe;
> she cherished me upon my mother's breast.
> When I stammer, she forms the words in my mouth,
> and when I am silent, she has understood my thoughts.
> If I shout and rage, she hears my plea and my
>   uncertainty.

When I am afraid, she stays close to me,
and when I am full of terror, she does not hide her face.
If I struggle against her, she will contain me,
and when I resist her, she will match my strength.

But if I am complacent, she confronts me;
when I cling to falsehood, she undermines my pride;
for she is jealous for my integrity,
and her longing is for nothing less than truth.

To all who are weak, she shows compassion,
and those who are downtrodden, she causes to rise.
But she will confound the arrogant
at the height of their power,
and the oppressor she will throw to the ground;
the strategies of the hard-hearted she will utterly
    confute.

God pities the fallen, and I will love her;
she challenges the mighty,
and I desire her with my whole heart.
God is the rock in whom I put my trust,
and all my meaning is contained in her;
for without God there is no security,
and apart from her there is no place of safety. (29)

As a woman in labour

As a woman in labour who longs for the birth,
I long for you, O God;
as she is weary to see the face of her child,
so do I seek your deliverance.
She cries out, she pants, because her pain is great,
and her longing is beyond measure;
her whole body is groaning in travail
until she shall be delivered.

My soul hungers for you
as the child for her mother's breast;
like the infant who cries out in the night,
who waits in the dark to be comforted.
At night I will cry for your justice,
and in the morning I will seek you early;
for you, O God, are the source of my salvation,
and all my nourishment is found in you.

As a woman looks to her friend,
that she may open her heart and be free,
that her words may find understanding,
and her fears may be contained;
so do I look to you, O God,
that you may search me and know my ways,
bringing me judgement and tenderness
and sending me home released.

As the body of the lover yearns for her beloved,
so is my desire for your touch.
She cries out from her depths, she weeps,
and cannot speak
because of the beauty of her beloved.
You also have laid your hand upon me,
and I cannot forget your ways.

So I will cry for my Beloved and will not rest,
until I dwell in the darkness of her embrace,
and all my silence is enclosed in her.   (29)

Welcoming home a new baby

(The family gathers round the pram/cot in which the baby is lying.)

LEADER You, Lord are the source of all life.
ALL   Glory to you, O God.

LEADER You have given us *N*.
ALL   Glory to you, O God.
LEADER You share with us the work of creation.
ALL   Glory to you, O God.
LEADER Let us remember how God, in Jesus, came into the
         world as a baby.

A reading from Luke 2.16–20

> The shepherds hurried away and found Mary and
> Joseph, and the baby lying in a manger. When they saw
> the child, they repeated what they had been told about
> him, and everyone who heard it was astonished at what
> the shepherds had to say. As for Mary, she treasured all
> these things and pondered them in her heart. And the
> shepherds went back glorifying and praising God for all
> they had heard and seen.

A prayer

> With joy, Lord, we lovingly welcome *N* into his/her
> home. May he/she feel safe here and know that he/she is
> loved by us all. Touch him/her with your love and with
> the beauty and wonder of living.   **Amen.**

The Lord's Prayer

> Our Father . . .

Prayer

LEADER Angels sang at the birth of Jesus.
ALL   We celebrate the birth of *N*.
LEADER Shepherds marvelled at the birth of Jesus.
ALL   We celebrate the birth of *N*.
LEADER Wise men knelt in worship before Jesus.
ALL   We celebrate the birth of *N*.

Reading

> The star they had seen in the east went ahead of them until it stopped in the place where the child was. When they saw the star, they were overjoyed. On coming into the house, they saw the child with his mother, Mary, and they bowed down and worshipped him. Then they opened their treasures and presented him with gifts of gold, frankincense and myrrh.

Matthew 2.9–11

(Presents or cards may be placed round the baby's cot.)

A prayer

The mother may read (adapted from 1 Samuel 1.27–28)
MOTHER I prayed for this child and the Lord has granted me what I asked of him. So I now give him/her to the Lord.

Everyone stretches out a hand towards the baby.
LEADER May the joy of the angels,
        the enthusiasm of the shepherds,
        the perseverance of the wise men
        and the peace of the Christ child
        be with you, *N*, and remain with you always.   (38)

Miscarriage

A short service for use in hospital, soon after the event

(If the parents wish, hospital staff, family members or friends may be asked to be present.)

> Now the word of the Lord came to me, saying, 'Before I formed you in the womb, I knew you and before I formed you in the womb, I consecrated you.'
>
> *Jeremiah 1.4–5*

(A candle may be lit and parents or others may say something or place a gift near it if they wish.)

Prayers for the baby

> God of compassion,
> you make nothing in vain,
> and love all that you have created,
> we commend to you *N* and *N*'s child (*name child if appropriate*)
> for whom they pour out such great love,
> for whom they cherished many hopes and dreams.
> Grant them the assurance that their child,
> though not seen by us, is seen and known by you,
> and will share the risen life of your Son, Jesus Christ.
> **Amen.**   (18)

Reading

> The lamb who is at the heart of the throne will be their shepherd and will guide them to the springs of the water of life; and God will wipe away all tears from their eyes.
>
> *Revelation 7.17*

O Father of all,
we pray to you for those we love but do not see.
Grant them your peace;
let light perpetual shine on them;
and in your loving wisdom,
work in them the good purpose of your perfect will
through Jesus Christ our Lord.   **Amen.**

A prayer for the mother

O God, the giver of all comfort,
look down on *N* who has known the joy of a new
   life within,
and the desolation of losing that life;
do not hide your face from her distress,
but hear her when she calls to you;
restore her to health in body and spirit
and renew in her hope, faith and love,
for the sake of your Son who brought peace to
   the grieving hearts of mothers,
Jesus Christ our Lord.   **Amen.**   (18)

A prayer for the family

Loving God,
be with us as we face the mystery of life and death.
Strengthen the bonds of this family (*name if desired*)
as they bear their loss.
Help them to go on from here
with courage and confidence in your care and love;
through our Redeemer, Jesus Christ.   **Amen.**   (5)

Blessing

> Unto God's gracious care we commit you,
> May the Lord bless you and watch over you,
> May the Lord make his face to shine upon you,
> May the Lord look kindly on you and give you peace,
> now and for ever. **Amen.**

Still birth

A short service for use in hospital soon after the birth

(*If the parent(s) wish, family members, hospital staff or friends may be invited to be present. The baby may be dressed and laid in a crib or held, according to the parents' wishes.*)

> Now the word of the Lord came to me, saying, 'Before I formed you in the womb, I knew you and before you were born, I consecrated you.'
>
> *Jeremiah 1.4–5*

Naming

(*The parents may name the child, saying the words themselves or having the minister say them.*)

> *N*, I/we give you this name; know that you are a child of God, Father, Son and Holy Spirit.

(*A candle may be lit. The parents or others may say something or place gifts near the child.*)

> *N*, I/we give you this light/gift; know that you are precious in our sight.

Prayers of commendation

> God of compassion, you make nothing in vain
> and love all you have created;
> we commend to you *N* and *N*'s child, *N,*
> for whom they pour out such great love,
> for whom they cherished so many hopes and dreams.
> We had longed to welcome him/her amongst us;
> Grant us the assurance that he/she is now encircled in
>   your arms of love,
> and shares the resurrection life of your Son, Jesus Christ.
> **Amen.** (5)

Reading

> The Lamb who is at the heart of the throne will be their
> shepherd and will guide them to the springs of the water
> of life; and God will wipe away all tears from their eyes.
> *Revelation 7.17*

Reading

> There is nothing in death or life, in the world as it is, or
> the world as it shall be, nothing in all creation that can
> separate us from the love of God in Jesus Christ our Lord.
> *Romans 8.38–39*

Prayer

> Father of all,
> though we had wished with all our hearts
> to keep *N* with us,
> we now entrust him/her
> to your protection and keeping,

to rest in peace eternally,
through Jesus Christ our Saviour.   **Amen.**   (18)

A prayer for the mother

O God, the giver of all comfort,
look down on *N*,
who has endured the pains of birth without its joys;
do not hide your face from her distress,
but hear her when she calls to you in sorrow;
restore her to health in body, relieving her pain;
dispel the darkness which surrounds her
at the loss of this precious child,
who lived within her and inspired hope and love;
this we ask through Jesus Christ our Lord.   **Amen.**   (18)

A prayer for the family

Loving God,
be with us as we face the mystery of life and death.
Strengthen the bonds of this family (*name if desired*)
as they bear their loss.
Today they come to you in shock and confusion,
help them to find peace
in the knowledge of your loving mercy to all your
children,
and send your light to guide them out of darkness
into the assurance of your love.   **Amen.**   (5)

A blessing

May Christ, who out of despair
brings new hope and a new future,
fill you with his strength;
and the blessing. . .   (18)

Emergency baptism

This service is intended for use when a child is very ill and the parents desire baptism. It is usually taken by the hospital chaplain, but can be used by any Christian person. At the baptism, water is poured three times. The priest in charge of the parish in which the child's parents live should normally be informed that the baptism has taken place. Family members and hospital staff may be invited to take part in the service, if the parents wish.

It is not always appropriate to offer baptism under these circumstances and it might be more suitable to provide prayers and a blessing.

The introduction

> In the Gospel, Jesus tells us that unless we have been born again we cannot see the kingdom of God. God gives us the way to a second birth, a new creation and life in union with him. Baptism is the sign and seal of this new birth. (On one occasion when children were being brought to Jesus some of his followers tried to keep them away, but Jesus welcomed the children in love, took them in his arms, and blessed them, saying, 'Let the children come to me; do not try to stop them; for the kingdom of God belongs to such as these.'**)

(**For pastoral reasons, it may be advisable to omit these words in the case of a terminally ill child, if the minister has not had much time to speak to the parents about their understanding of baptism. Parents have sometimes taken these words to imply that Jesus desires the death of their baby.)

> Let us pray for this child whom we bring, in love, to baptism in the name of our Lord.

Heavenly Father,
grant that by your Holy Spirit
this child may be born again
and surrounded by your love
in the family of your Church,
through Jesus Christ our Lord.   **Amen.**

The signing

I sign you with the sign of the cross to show that you are
a member of Christ's family and loved by him.

The blessing of the water

Heavenly Father, we ask you to bless this water that
he/she who is washed in it may be made one with Christ.
Send your Holy Spirit upon him/her to bring him/her to
new birth in the family of your church in heaven and on
earth, and raise him/her, with Christ, to full and eternal
life.

The baptism

N, I baptize you in the name of the Father and of the Son
and of the Holy Spirit.   **Amen.**

The Lord's Prayer

Our Father . . .

*(Prayers for the child, the parents and family may be added, followed
by the grace or a blessing.)*   (39)

4

Relationships

Engagement

Creator God, you have sown in the hearts of *N* and *N*
the seeds of longing and affection that they might grow
together in mutual trust and love.
Bless the commitment they have made to each other;
Bless this ring that it may be a sign of their hopes for
    each other;
Bless this time of preparation that they may rejoice with
    their family and friends on the day of their wedding
and in company with Christ our Lord. **Amen.** (19)

Eternal God,
give your blessing to *N* and *N*
in their hopes and in their dreams.
May these come true
through their faith in each other
and their trust in you.
Teach them how great is the joy
that comes from sharing;
how deep the love that grows with giving.
Lead them in peace
to the day of their wedding
and be with them in their hearts and in their home(s)
now and for ever. (19)

The renewal of marriage vows

This order may be used at an anniversary, or after a time of separation or difficulty in a marriage, or at a new beginning. It can also be used at a service where a number of couples reaffirm their marriage.

Whilst normally taking place in church, this service or prayers from it could be used in other appropriate places.

(There may be introductory music, during which the couple enter the church, and a hymn may be sung.)

Scripture sentences

> God is love, and those who live in love
> live in God, and God lives in them.   *1 John 4.16*

> Unless the Lord builds the house, those who labour
> build in vain.   *Psalm 127.1*

MINISTER God our Father,
> You have taught us through your Son
> that love is the fulfilling of the law.
> Grant to your servants
> that, loving one another,
> they may continue in your love until their lives' end:
> through Jesus Christ our Lord. **Amen.**   (9)

MINISTER Marriage is God's gift to us,
> to help man and woman find companionship, help and
>   comfort.
> It is a means of grace, in which husband and wife,
> living faithfully together, may find the fulfilment of
> human love in tenderness and respect.
> In Christian marriage God makes his servants one.

Their life together is a witness to his love in this troubled world, a love by which unity overcomes division, forgiveness heals injury, and joy triumphs over sorrow.

By marriage God enriches society and strengthens the sanctity of family life by providing homes which may be trusted with the gift and care of children.
Our Lord Jesus Christ hallowed marriage by his presence at a wedding in Cana of Galilee, and it is consecrated as the symbol of the union between Christ and his Church.
X and Y are here today to celebrate their marriage and to reaffirm their commitment to this way of life which God has provided and Christ has blessed.
We rejoice with them, and support them with our prayers. (21)

(Other openings, such as that in The Alternative Service Book Marriage Service, may also be adapted here.)

X + Y   God our Father,
we thank you for the marriage
you have given us.
We rejoice in all that has been good
and ask your forgiveness
on anything that has been amiss.
Renew us by your Spirit,
inspire us with your love,
and refresh us in love for one another. **Amen.** (17)

Reading(s)
Address

MINISTER   X, you have taken Y to be your wife.
Will you continue to love her, comfort her, honour and protect her, and forsaking all others, be faithful to her as long as you both shall live?

X.   I will.

MINISTER   Y, you have taken X to be your husband.
            Will you continue to love him, comfort him, honour
            and protect him, and forsaking all others, be faithful
            to him as long as you both shall live?

Y.   I will.

(*The couple take each other's hands.*)

X.   I, X, renew my promise
            to take you, Y,
            to be my wife.
            To have and to hold,
            from this day forward,
            for better, for worse,
            for richer, for poorer,
            in sickness and in health,
            to love, cherish and worship,
            till death us do part,
            according to God's holy law,
            and this is my solemn vow.

Y.   I, Y, renew my promise
            to take you, X,
            to be my husband.
            To have and to hold,
            from this day forward,
            for better, for worse,
            for richer, for poorer,
            in sickness and in health,
            to love, cherish and obey,
            till death us do part,
            according to God's holy law,
            and this is my solemn vow.

Or

X.   I, X, in the presence of God
            renew my commitment
            to you, Y, as your husband.

        All that I am I give to you,
        and all that I have I share with you.
        Whatever the future holds
        I will love you
        and stand by you as long as we both shall live.

Y.   I, Y, in the presence of God
        renew my commitment
        to you, X, as your wife.
        All that I am I give to you,
        and all that I have I share with you.
        Whatever the future holds
        I will love you
        and stand by you as long as we both shall live.   (21)

(If new rings are to be used, this prayer follows:)

MINISTER Heavenly Father, by your blessing let these new rings
        be to X and Y a symbol of unending love and
        faithfulness, to remind them of the renewal of the
        vows they have made this day; through Jesus Christ
        our Lord. **Amen.**

(The new rings are exchanged.)

(This prayer may be used by each person.)

        I give you this ring
        as a sign of the renewal of our marriage.
        In thanksgiving, and in love
        I offer you all that I am
        within the love of God
        Father, Son and Holy Spirit.   (17)

MINISTER God the Father,
        God the Son,
        God the Holy Spirit,
        bless, preserve and keep you;
        the Lord mercifully grant you the riches of his grace,
        that you may please him both in body and in soul,
        and, living together in faith and love,

may receive the blessings of eternal life.   **Amen.**   (9)

Affirmation by the people

MINISTER   Will you, family and friends of X and Y,
who have gathered here today, continue to support
them in their marriage?
PEOPLE   We will.

Prayers

MINISTER   Lord and Saviour Jesus Christ,
who shared at Nazareth the life of an earthly home,
reign in the home of these your servants as Lord
and King;
give them grace to minister to others
as you have ministered to them,
and grant that by deed and word
they may be witnesses of your saving love
to those among whom they live;
for the sake of your holy name.   **Amen.**   (9)

Almighty God, giver of life and love, bless X and Y
whom you have joined in Christian marriage. Grant
them wisdom and devotion in their life together, that
each may be to the other a strength in need, a comfort in
sorrow, and a companion in joy. So unite their wills in
your will, and their spirits in your Spirit, that they live
and grow together in love and peace all the days of their
life, through Jesus Christ our Lord.   **Amen.**   (9)

Generous God,
your Son has shown us how to love
and invites us to love each other as he loves us.

We pray for X and Y,
with their shared memories of the past;
of joy and laughter,
sadness and disappointment,
forgiving and being forgiven.
Grant that they might put their trust in you
to guide and guard them for the future. (21)

X + Y   God of tenderness and strength,
you have brought our paths together
and led us to this day;
go with us now as we travel through good times,
through trouble or through change.
Bless our home, our partings and our meetings.
Make us worthy of each other's best,
and tender with each other's dreams,
trusting in your love in Jesus Christ. **Amen.** (5)

Blessing

God the Holy Trinity,
make you strong in faith and love,
defend you on every side,
and guide you in truth and peace;
and the blessing of God almighty,
the Father, the Son, and the Holy Spirit,
be among you and remain with you always. **Amen.** (9)

Or

May God the Father give you joy;
may God the Son give you grace;
may God the Holy Spirit
fill your hearts with love.

And the blessing of God almighty,
Father, Son, and Holy Spirit,

be upon you and abide in you,
now and always.   **Amen.**   (21)

Blessing of a ring

Eternal God,
hear our prayer for *N* and *N*
as we give you thanks
for the life they have embraced together
and the happiness they have known.
Bless this ring
that it may be to them
a sign of their unending
love and faithfulness.
And as the years go by
bring them ever closer
to each other and to you
for Jesus Christ's sake.   **Amen.**   (19)

Prayers for lone parents

Jesus, son of Mary,
born into a poor family,
you shared the pressure of daily living.
We pray for *N*
as at each moment he/she looks to create a place
where relationships are secure,
where his/her children are given love,
where food and shelter are provided.

Lord God,
as a Father you care for your children;
as a Mother you lead your young.
Be Father and Mother here.
So fill this place with your presence

that no one lacks the knowledge of love,
and all grow in dignity, worth, and stature.
Provide for all their needs,
and give each one the space to grow,
and the cause to rejoice in the joy of heaven.
For your name's sake.   **Amen.**   (17)

For a lone mother

Loving Jesus,
cared for by a mother,
you know the strains of life in a home.
We pray for *N*.
Bless her as she is a mother to her children (*names*)
and be for them all that she cannot be.
Surround her with the love of others,
that she too may know your tender care,
and find each day new cause for hope.
For your name's sake.   **Amen.**   (17)

For a lone father

Lord Jesus,
You taught us to call God 'Father'.
Bless *N*, father to his children (*names*).
As he is aware of what he cannot be,
so provide for him
that his children know a mother's care.
Be present in his home,
and in all family relationships,
so that day by day your love is revealed,
and their lives made whole.
For your name's sake.   **Amen.**   (17)

On leaving home

Lord Jesus Christ,
born at Bethlehem and nurtured in Nazareth,
give your grace to this family.
May *N* step into the world
with the confidence of their care
and in the strength of their love.
Keep them close to each other
that as *N* leaves in peace,
So may he/she be welcomed home
with joy.   **Amen.**   (19)

5

Endings and new beginnings

A liturgical framework for ending a group or organization

Introduction

Church and community activities and groups and the nature of their ending are extremely varied, and a ceremony marking their end will inevitably be a 'one off'.

We are usually better at celebrating beginnings than acknowledging endings, but endings are a necessary and valuable part of life. God is continually at work in creation, and human beings therefore generate changes and perceive new opportunities. To end well is to be better prepared for a new beginning. It is also to value and respect what has been. The Christian Gospel speaks of death giving rise to new life.

The following therefore is mainly a guide to clarifying what you want to do, with some choices and resources available.

Aims for a ceremony of ending

To give thanks and make remembrance for all that has been achieved and all that it has meant for people.   (Past)
To draw near to God to express mourning and relief, disappointment, anger, and even feelings of betrayal: to let go.   (Present)
To look to the future, and identify new possibilities, with an appropriate expression of hope.   (Future)

Structure of the service

The preparation
- Introduction to the group and the purpose of the ceremony/service
- Sentence of Scripture, and motto of the organization
- Collect

The Word
- Reading(s) from the Bible
- Shared silence, and symbolic gesture
- Commendation: formal or informal sharing and valuing of memories and blessings of the group

Prayers
- Prayers of thanksgiving, penitence, intercession
- The Lord's Prayer

Conclusion
- Grace, Blessing, and Commission
- Something to take away

Resources

Reading

> Forgetting what lies behind, and straining forward to what lies ahead, I press on toward the goal for the prize of the heavenly call of God in Christ Jesus.
>
> *Philippians 3.13–14, NRSV*

Collect

Living God, ever behind us and ever before us,
in creation you give us a life which is always changing.
In our beginning and ending,
in our living and dying,
strengthen our confidence in you,
that in all the changes and chances of this world,
we may rest on your eternal changelessness.
Through Jesus Christ our Lord. **Amen.**   (17)

The Word

For everything there is a season, and a time for every
matter under heaven:

a time to be born, and a time to die;
a time to plant, and a time to pluck up what is planted;

a time to kill, and a time to heal;
a time to break down and a time to build up;

a time to weep and a time to laugh;
a time to mourn and a time to dance;

a time to throw away stones and a time to gather stones
   together;
a time to embrace, and a time to refrain from
   embracing;

a time to seek and a time to lose;
a time to keep, and a time to throw away;

a time to tear and a time to sew;
a time to keep silence and a time to speak;

a time to love and a time to hate;
a time for war and a time for peace.

Ecclesiastes 3.1–8, NRSV

Jesus said: 'No one sews a piece of unshrunk cloth on an old cloak; otherwise, the patch pulls away from it, the new from the old, and a worse tear is made. And no one puts new wine into old wineskins; otherwise, the wine will burst the skins, and the wine is lost, and so are the skins; but one puts new wine into fresh wineskins.'

Mark 2.21–22, NRSV

Other readings
Psalm 23; Psalm 103;
Deuteronomy 34.1–2a, 4–12; Luke 6.20–28; Luke 10.38–42; Luke 17.7–10; 1 Corinthians 3.5–17; 2 Corinthians 4.7–18; Philippians 2.1–11; Philippians 3.7–14; Colossians 1.15–20; Hebrews 11.8–16.

Silence and action
- Silent remembrance
- Sharing the Peace
- Use of the group symbol, to touch or look at
- Closing the Book
- Extinguishing a candle, and lighting another
- Presenting a cheque winding up the accounts to another organization.

Prayers
- Specific thanksgivings with responses (e.g. 'Gracious Lord, we thank you')
- Penitential material
- Intercessions, beginning with 'Compassionate God ...', and covering past, present, and future.

Collects and other prayers
ASB: Epiphany 2, 4, 9 before Easter, Lent 3, Palm Sunday, Easter
Day 2nd, Easter 4, Pentecost 1, 10, 11, 18, 19, St Barnabas.
(All adapted)

Prayers

Go before us, O Lord, in all our doings
with your most gracious favour,
and further us with your continual help;
that in all our works,
begun, continued, and ended in you,
we may glorify your holy name
and finally by your mercy
obtain everlasting life;
through Jesus Christ our Lord.   **Amen.**   (20)

O God of comfort and challenge
whose presence is ever reliable
and ever unexpected:
grant us to grieve over what is ending
without falling into despair
and to enter our new vocation
without forgetting your voice,
through Jesus Christ.   **Amen.**   (29)

From the flowing of the tide
To its ebbing
From the waxing of life
To its waning
Of your Peace provide us
Of your Light lead us
Of your Goodness give us
Of your Grace grant us
Of your Power protect us
Of your Love lift us

And in your arms accept us.
From the ebbing of the tide
To its flowing
From the waxing of life
To its waning.   (25)

Gracious and Holy Father
give us wisdom to perceive you,
intelligence to understand you
diligence to seek you,
patience to wait for you,
eyes to behold you,
a heart to meditate on you,
and a life to proclaim you.   (30)

Let nothing disturb you, nothing dismay you; all things
pass, but God never changes. Whoever has God lacks
nothing: if you only have God you have more than
enough.   *St Teresa*

For all that has been, thanks.
To all that shall be, yes.
At all times and in all places.   (31)

Blessings

Christ the Alpha and Omega,
the beginning and the end,
give you strength to do his will,
and confidence in the completeness of his love,
And the blessing . . .   (17)

May Christ who out of defeat
brings new hope and a new future
fill you with his new life.
And the blessing . . .   (5)

May Christ's holy, healing, and enabling Spirit
  be with you
and guide you on your way at every change
  and turn.
And the blessing . . .   (7)

May the God of hope fill us
with all joy and peace in believing
through the power of the Holy Spirit.
And the blessing . . .   (7)

Ascension

Christ our king make you faithful and strong
  to do his will,
that you may reign with him in glory;
and the blessing . . .   (9)

Trinity

God the Holy Trinity make you strong in faith and love,
defend you on every side,
and guide you in truth and peace;
and the blessing . . .   (9)

To take away

- Commemorative service sheet
- Group photograph

Acknowledging the ending of a relationship

An unpleasant fact of human existence is that relationships, including marriages, end, because the strain placed upon them is too great. Whilst recognizing that God's ideal is that this should not be, it is preferable to recognize an ending rather than hide a failure. 'There is a great need to face up formally to failure and tie up loose ends in order to be able to start again . . . The Church has failed to provide liturgical opportunities for those going through a parting to make sense of their experience' (Elizabeth Stuart). William Willimon says: 'the Church has been given the awesome power to loose as well as bind.'

These prayers are offered to allow those in a relationship which has come to an end to affirm all that has been good, to acknowledge its formal ending, and to play their part in its new status, especially where there are responsibilities to be carried out, such as the care of children. These prayers can be used where only one partner is present, as an act of restoration, or where both are present, as a formal act of separation and commitment to a new future.

Reading

> For everything there is a season, and a time for every matter under heaven: a time to break down, and a time to build up; a time to weep and a time to mourn.
>
> *Ecclesiastes 3.1, 3–4*

Introduction

> We have come today out of love for N (and N), to mark the end of their commitment to one another, to recognize their grief at this ending, and to pray for them as they embark on this stage of their lives. So we pray for God's blessing on them now and in the days to come.   (17)

Recognition of failure

MINISTER When a relationship ends there is a kind of death. Our hopes for that relationship, our vision of the future, our promise of lifelong commitment all die.

O God, we wonder whether we were wrong in our beginnings, or wrong in our endings.

We believe that we have faced things that were too great for us, and know that you never ask us to be destroyed.

In Christ you entered all the painful experiences of life. We confess that in the complexities of human relationship, we have failed, and have wounded those we sought to love.

In silence we make our own confession to you.
(*Silence*)
Forgive us, O God.

BOTH   Forgive us and help us, O God.

Hope and promise

To God our endings can be the sign of new beginnings.
Our deaths can be the prelude to the resurrection.
We bear the consequences of what we do but we are not
    condemned.

Receive the gift of new life,
and the sign that even at this moment you are one with
    Christ,
who will never leave you or forsake you, to the end of
    time.   (32)

Prayer for restoration (where one partner is present)

In the name of the God who brings hope out of defeat,
and life out of death,
we pray for *N*, wounded at the end of this relationship.
Anoint him with the oil of healing,
fill him with the power of the resurrection,

enable him to look to your future for him,
safe in the knowledge of your never failing love.   (17)

Prayer of St Teresa

N, let nothing disturb you,
nothing destroy you;
all things pass, but God never changes.
Whoever has God lacks nothing;
if you only have God, you have more than enough.

Act of separation (where both partners are present)
(Each partner in turn)

I, *N*, hereby affirm my place in this ending of our commitment. From this day our lives separate, and our loves
part.
Now I enter into a new relationship with you. I shall treasure the things we shared that were beautiful, and I shall
hold as valuable and worthy the new and happy things in
your future life.
We have hurt and been hurt. Knowing your strengths
and weaknesses, I shall see and honour and treat you as a
person.
This is my pledge.

*(There may be symbolic action, including the returning of rings or
gifts, and the handing over of shared possessions.)*

Pronouncement of separation

MINISTER *N* and *N* have stated their intention to live apart and
to create lives independent of one another. They have
declared their common commitment to each other's
health and well being, and to that of all their lives

will touch. They have made pledges of trustworthiness, respecting themselves and each other.

Their commitment is dissolved.

I summon them in the name of God the maker of love, the pain bearer and bringer of forgiveness to look to the hope of the resurrection in the dark days that lie ahead.

I summon their families and friends to respect this decision, and to mediate the love, forgiveness and grace of God to them in the coming days.

Do you promise to do so?

ALL   We do.   (33)

Act of recognition

N (and *N*),
your marriage was blessed before God,
and in God's presence we recognize that your marriage
    has ended.
We now affirm you as living singly,
and pledge to give you our support
as you continue to seek God's help and guidance for
    your new life.

Prayers

O God, our comfort and challenge,
whose presence is ever reliable
and ever unexpected;
grant us to grieve over what is ending,
without ever falling into despair,
and to enter on our new vocation

without forgetting your voice,
through Jesus Christ.   **Amen.**   (29)

Gracious God,
in you we see the promise of all that is new.
We pray for all who grieve a loss in their lives today;
may they be comforted.
We pray for all who are bowed down
by guilt and pain,
and for all who look to the future with fear and
    loneliness;
may they experience your loving presence.
Hold them safe by the rock of your faithfulness to us
throughout the ages.   (32)

A prayer for family and friends

Faithful God,
many people feel diminished by this ending.
Some will not be reconciled to it,
and many will grieve.
Be their comfort and support,
and allow them to face this new life
with hope for their future.
In the name of Christ.   **Amen.**   (17)

A prayer for children

God our Father and Mother,
we pray for *N,* children of this marriage now ended.
Let them adjust to this new state,
heal the wounds of separation,
and dispel the false guilt
which places blame at the wrong door.

Be their strength and support,
that they may live in good relationship
with each parent.
In the name of Christ.   **Amen.**   (17)

Blessing

God who brings light out of darkness,
order out of chaos,
wholeness out of brokenness,
life out of death,
bless us with your transforming love
now and throughout life's endings.   **Amen.**   (34)

End of working life

Facing retirement

Lord, as *N* looks toward retirement
we thank you for the blessings of past years.
Help him/her to adjust to a different lifestyle;
to grasp the new opportunities given,
and to remember the needs of others.
May *N* use his/her leisure creatively,
and in the newfound joy of time to spend,
may he/she continue in your love and service.
Through Jesus Christ our Lord.   **Amen.**   (27)

Creator God,
you made from nothing all that is
and you give us grace to find fulfilment in our work;
hear our prayer for *N* in his/her retirement
that he/she may graciously relinquish what is past
and gladly accept new opportunities still to come.

We thank you for work that is done and pray
that these years of experience may not be wasted
but used in your service for Jesus Christ's sake.   (19)

O God our Father, today we look back across the
working life of *N*,
soon to come to an end.
There is so much for which he/she seeks forgiveness:
For wasted time, for neglected opportunities, for
attention given to wrong things, for mistakes made:
Forgive him/her O God.

There is so much for which *N* gives thanks:
For health and strength, for protection in the time of
danger, for healing in the time of illness, for upholding
in the day of sorrow, for daily light and daily leading:
Thank you O God.

We pray today in trust that *N*'s work was begun and has
continued in you. As this stage of his/her life now finds
its end, we pray that you will guide him/her with your
gracious favour, and further him/her with your
continual help.
Through Jesus Christ our Lord.   **Amen.**   (36)

Blessing for one laying down office

May the God who rested on the seventh day
to delight in all her creation
hold you in her arms
as you have held this work,
celebrate with us
the life that takes life from you
and give you grace to let go
into a new freedom.   (29)

6

Preparation for the sacraments: baptism and Holy Communion

Prayer before communion

> Almighty God,
> by your grace alone
> we are accepted and called to your service:
> You have cleansed and renewed us in the water of
>   baptism,
> you have set your seal upon us with the gift of your
>   Spirit:
> Nourish us, we pray, in the bread and wine
> by which Jesus commanded us to remember him,
> that we may be living members of your Son,
> strengthened, with your whole church,
> to exercise the ministry to which we are called,
> to your honour and glory.   **Amen.**   (18)

Prayers before baptism *(for use with candidates)*

> Gracious God, as *N* prepares to enter the waters of
>   baptism,
> we pray, through your Son Jesus Christ, that you will
> deliver him/her from the old way of sin and death,
> open his/her heart to your grace and truth,
> and fill him/her with your holy and life-giving Spirit:
> Teach him/her to love others in the power of the Spirit,

and live a life which speaks of the coming of your
   Kingdom,
to your eternal honour and glory.   **Amen.**   (18)

For those about to be baptized

(*For use especially on days which precede public services of Holy
Baptism, and at other times at the discretion of the minister.*)

Lord Jesus Christ, you desire that everyone who follows
   you
shall be born again by water and the Spirit:
Remember your servants (*here they may be named*)
   who are soon to
be baptized in your Name.

By their names, Lord:
Grant that you will know them and call them to a life
   of service.   **Amen.**
Grant that they may become the persons you created
   them to be.   **Amen.**
Grant that they may be written for ever in your Book of
   Life.   **Amen.**

Through the water of their baptism, Lord:
Grant that they may be united with you in your death.
   Amen.
Grant that they may receive forgiveness of all their sins.
   Amen.
Grant that they may have power to endure, and strength
   to have the victory in the battle of life.   **Amen.**

As members of your church, Lord:

Grant that they may rise to a new life in the fellowship of those who love you. **Amen.**

Grant that they may suffer when another suffers and, when another rejoices, rejoice. **Amen.**

Grant that they may be your faithful soldiers and servants until their life's end. **Amen.**

Through the abiding presence of your Spirit, Lord:

Grant that they may lead the rest of their lives according to this beginning. **Amen.**

Grant that when they pass through the dark waters of death, you will be with them. **Amen.**

Grant that they may inherit the kingdom of glory prepared for them from the foundation of the world. **Amen.** (26)

7

Healing and wholeness

The ministry to the sick

The Church's work of healing is an important part of her ministry in the world. Both the laying-on of hands and anointing with oil are ancient practices by which God's healing power is shown to those who are anxious or sick. Some people may be happier to use one or other of the two rites; though it is quite usual to use both.

In episcopal churches, it is customary that whenever possible the oil should be that blessed by the bishop. For situations where this is not possible, there is appended to this rite a prayer for the blessing of oil.

It is not always necessary or appropriate that anointing and the laying-on of hands should be followed by the reception of Holy Communion. When this does occur, it is desirable that the forms of words should be brief.

Generally, whenever possible, this rite should be celebrated gently with time for reflection; it will be most fitting that moments of silence are included at various points.

Sentences

> Peace be to this house and to all who dwell in it.

Or

> In the Name of the Father and of the Son and of the Holy Spirit.

Penitential prayers

Confession

MINISTER Lord Jesus, you healed the sick: Lord, have mercy.
ALL   Lord, have mercy.
MINISTER Lord Jesus, you forgave sinners: Christ have mercy.
ALL   Christ, have mercy.
MINISTER Lord Jesus, you give us yourself to heal us and bring
             us strength: Lord, have mercy.
ALL   Lord, have mercy.   (1)

Absolution

God, the Father of mercies, has reconciled the world to
himself through the death and resurrection of his Son,
Jesus Christ, not counting our trespasses, but sending his
Holy Spirit to shed abroad his love among us. By the
ministry of reconciliation entrusted by Christ to his
Church, receive his pardon and peace to stand before him
in his strength alone God this day and evermore.   (2)

Collect
(*when there is anointing*)

God of Heaven and earth, you anointed your Son with
the Holy Spirit and with power to bring to us the blessings of your kingdom. Anoint your Church with the
same Holy Spirit, that we who share in Jesus' suffering
and victory may bear witness to the Gospel of salvation;
through Jesus Christ.   (1)

O God of peace, who taught us that in returning and rest
we shall be saved, in quietness and confidence shall be our

strength; by the might of your Spirit lift us now to your presence, where we may be still and know that you are God; through Jesus Christ. (3)

Reading

Jesus spoke these words: 'Everything is entrusted to me by my Father; and no one knows the Son but the Father, and no one knows the Father but the Son and those to whom the Son chooses to reveal him.

'Come to me, all who are weary and whose load is heavy; I will give you rest. Take my yoke upon you and learn from me, for I am gentle and humble-hearted; and you will find rest for your souls. For my yoke is easy to wear and my load is light.'

Matthew 11.25, 27–30, REB

Or

There was a woman who had suffered from hae-morrhages for twelve years; and nobody had been able to cure her. She came up from behind and touched the edge of Jesus' cloak and at once her haemorrhage stopped. Jesus said, 'Who was it touched me?' All disclaimed it, and Peter said, 'Master, the crowds are hemming you in and pressing upon you!' But Jesus said, 'Someone did touch me, for I felt that power had gone out from me.' Then the woman, seeing that she was detected, came trembling and fell at his feet. Before all the people she explained why she had touched him and how she had been cured instantly. He said to her, 'Daughter, your faith has healed you. Go in peace.'

Luke 8.43–48, REB

Laying-on of hands and anointing

Introduction

We are gathered here in the Name of our Lord Jesus Christ, who is present among us. As the Gospels relate, the sick came to him for healing; moreover, he loves us so much that he died for our sake. Through the Apostle James, he has commanded us: 'Are there any who are sick among you? Let them send for the elders of the Church, and let them pray over them, anointing them with oil in the Name of the Lord; and the prayer of faith will save the sick persons. The Lord will raise them up; and if they have committed any sins, their sins will be forgiven.' Let us, therefore, commend our sick brother/sister *N* to the grace and power of Christ, that he may save him/her and raise him/her up.   (4)

Intercessions

MINISTER Like the first disciples before the coming of God's power at Pentecost, we wait in faith and pray.

(Silence)

Come, Lord, with your love and mercy in this ministry, and comfort *N* in his/her distress and free him/her from harm:

ALL Lord, hear our prayer.

MINISTER Relieve his/her suffering: sustain him/her with your power.

ALL Lord, hear our prayer.

MINISTER Give new strength to his/her body, mind and spirit.

ALL Lord, hear our prayer.

MINISTER As we lay hands on [and anoint] *N,* give him/her the assurance of your presence, and your peace.

ALL Lord, hear our prayer.   (1)

Be with us, Holy Spirit; pour your love into our hearts.
Be with us as of old, fill us with your power, direct all our
thoughts to your goodness.
Be present, Holy Spirit; bring faith and healing and
peace.   (5)

Laying-on of hands

In the Name of God most high we lay our hands upon
you. Receive Christ's healing touch to make you whole in
body, mind and spirit. The power of God strengthen you,
the love of God dwell in you and give you peace that you
may serve him now and evermore.   (5)

Anointing

N, I anoint you in the Name of the Father and of the Son
and of the Holy Spirit: as you are outwardly anointed
with this oil, so may God grant you inward anointing of
the Holy Spirit that you may find release from your suffering and be restored to wholeness and strength.   (6)

(after anointing)

N, lift up your face to the Light. The mark of Christ is
upon you; walk free and open your heart to life, for Christ
walks with you into a new day. **Amen.**   (35)

After the laying-on of hands and/or anointing

The almighty God, who is a strong tower for all who put
their trust in him, to whom all things in heaven, on earth,
and under the earth bow and obey, be now and evermore

your defence, and make you know and feel that the only name under heaven given for health and salvation, is the name of our Lord Jesus Christ.   (2)

Or
(*In extreme illness*)

Lord Jesus Christ, you chose to share our human nature, to redeem all people, and to heal the sick. Look with compassion upon your servant *N*, whom we have anointed in your Name with this holy oil for the healing of his/her body and spirit. Support him/her with your power, comfort him/her with your protection, and give him/her the strength to fight against evil. Since you have given him/her a share in your own Passion, help him/her to find hope in suffering, for you are Lord for ever and ever.   (4)

The Lord's Prayer

So in confidence let us pray to the Father for the coming of the kingdom among us:
Our Father . . .

(*Holy Communion may be received at this point.*)

Blessing

To God's gracious mercy and protection we commit you. The Lord bless you and watch over you, the Lord make his face to shine upon you and be gracious to you, the Lord look kindly on you and give you peace: and the blessing . . .

Blessing of oil

> O Lord, holy Father, giver of health and salvation: send
> Your Holy Spirit, we beseech you, to (bless and) sanctify
> this oil; that as your holy Apostles anointed many that
> were sick and healed them, so those who in faith and
> repentance receive this holy unction may be made whole:
> through Jesus Christ our Lord.   (6)

Communion at home

The practice of authorized people taking Holy Communion to
members of a church who are housebound is generally part of the
pastoral routine of a parish. Since it is the intention that by this
provision those who cannot be present at the Sunday Liturgy are
united with the worship that has been offered by those in church,
it is appropriate that the proper readings and prayers be those of
the Sunday or festival.

However, there are times either when there will be insufficient
opportunity to obtain the Sunday readings or when circumstances
suggest that some other prayers are more fitting. Provided here are
sets of prayers and readings for some such occasions.

At the communion of a sick person

Collect

> Heavenly Father,
> Giver of life and health:
> comfort and restore those who are sick,
> that they may be strengthened in their weakness
> and have confidence in your unfailing love;
> through Jesus Christ our Lord.   (9)

Reading

John, who was in prison, heard what Christ was doing, and sent his own disciples to put this question to him: 'Are you the one who is to come, or are we to expect someone else?' Jesus answered, 'Go and report to John what you hear and see: the blind recover their sight, the lame walk, lepers are made clean, the deaf hear, the dead are raised to life, the poor are brought good news.'

Matthew 11.2–5 REB

Or

Jesus spoke these words: 'Everything is entrusted to me by my Father; and no one knows the Son but the Father, and no one knows the Father but the Son and those to whom the Son chooses to reveal him.

'Come to me, all who are weary and whose load is heavy; I will give you rest. Take my yoke upon you and learn from me, for I am gentle and humble-hearted; and you will find rest for your souls, For my yoke is easy to wear and my load is light.'

Matthew 11.25, 27–30 REB

After communion

Loving and eternal God,
may this sacrament be for *N*
a lasting remedy for body and soul,
that he/she may live in him,
who has redeemed the whole world,
Jesus Christ our Lord.   (4)

At the communion of a dying person

Collect

God of Heaven,
into whose hands your Son Jesus Christ
commended his Spirit at his last hour:
into those same hands
we now commend your servant *N*
that death may be for him/her the gate to life
where he/she may enjoy eternal fellowship with you;
through Jesus Christ our Lord.   (16)

Reading

Jesus said, 'All that the Father gives me will come to me,
and anyone who comes to me I will not turn away. I have
come down from heaven, to do not my own will, but the
will of him who sent me. It is his will that I should not
lose even one of those he has given me, but should raise
them up on the last day. For it is my Father's will that
everyone who sees the Son and has faith in him should
have eternal life; and I will raise them up on the last day.'
John 6.37–40, REB

Or

Jesus said, 'Set your troubled hearts at rest. Trust in God
always; trust also in me. There are many dwelling-places
in my Father's house; if it were not so I should have told
you; for I am going to prepare a place for you. And if I go
and prepare a place for you, I shall come again and take
you to myself, so that where I am you may be also; and
you know the way I am taking.' Thomas said, 'Lord, we
do not know where you are going, so how can we know
the way?' Jesus replied, 'I am the way, the truth and the

life; no one comes to the Father except by me.'
John 14.1–6, REB

After communion

God of peace,
look with compassion on your servant *N*.
May this sacrament of Christ your Son
heal his/her soul that he/she may enter
your eternal kingdom.
Through Jesus Christ our Lord.   (14)

At the communion of a person in other circumstances

Collect

O God,
we thank you that in this wonderful sacrament
you have given us the memorial of your passion and
    death.
Grant us so to reverence
the sacred mysteries of your body and blood,
that we may know within ourselves
the fruits of your redemption:
who is alive and reigns with the Father and the Holy
    Spirit,
one God, now and for ever.

Reading

Jesus said, 'In very truth I tell you, unless you eat the flesh
of the son of man and drink his blood, you have no life in
you. Whoever eats my flesh and drinks my blood has
eternal life, and I will raise him up on that last day. My

flesh is real food: my blood is real drink. Whoever eats my flesh and drinks my blood dwells in me and I in him. As the living Father sent me, and I live because of the Father, so whoever eats me will live because of me. This is the bread which came down from heaven; it is not like the bread which our fathers ate: they are dead, but whoever eats this bread will live for ever.'

John 6.53–58, REB adapted

Or

Jesus said, 'I am the true vine and my Father is the gardener. Any branch of mine that is barren, he cuts away; and any fruiting branch he prunes clean, to make it more fruitful still. You are already clean because of the word I have spoken to you. Dwell in me, as I in you. No branch can bear fruit by itself, but only if it remains united with the vine; no more can you bear fruit, unless you remain united with me.

'I am the vine; you are the branches. Anyone who dwells in me, as I dwell in him, bears much fruit; apart from me you can do nothing.'

John 15.1–5, REB adapted

After communion

Eternal Father,
we thank you for refreshing us
with these heavenly gifts:
may our communion
strengthen us in faith
build us up in hope
and make us grow in love
for the sake of Jesus Christ our Lord.   (7)

A service for adults who have been abused as children

Some important points to think about.

This service was compiled by Bernice Broggio and Teresa Parker as a resource for adults who have been abused as children and their supporters. It may be used by such people as an aid to speaking about abuse and feeling the support of others which will assist in recovery. The service may be altered in any way that enables survivors to speak or recover.

The following guidelines will ensure the service helps rather than hinders the process of recovery.

Participants in the service should observe three simple principles: believe the survivor's story; say you are glad they told you; say the abuse was not their fault. The participants' agreement as to the confidentiality of what they will hear should be obtained.

Those arranging the service should prevent the following from happening:

- the use of this service without the consent of the survivor;
- intrusive questioning of the survivor before, within or after the service;
- touch, unless the survivor requests it;
- the use of any part of the service that the survivor is uncomfortable with;
- any suggestion that the service alone will provide a 'cure'.

Introduction

Collect

> God of the dispossessed,
> defender of the helpless,
> you grieve with all (women) who weep
> because their children are no more;
> may we also refuse to be comforted
> until the violence of the strong

has been confounded,
and the broken victims have been set free
in the name of Jesus Christ.   **Amen.**

We are here because *N* has been abused; her body, her feelings and her spirit have been injured. We are here to mourn with her and to cry out in anger with her. We are outraged at the exploitation of children and the distortion of sexuality into the violence that is all around us in patriarchal society.

We grieve because we do not know when the violence will end – but we refuse to give up.

We will not be intimidated and turned into fearful, guilty people. We believe that publicizing abuse destroys the evil power of secrecy and makes it easier for others to speak out, be heard and be made whole.

We love and affirm *N* who has been hurt.
Although she has been injured, she has not been destroyed.
Although she has been humiliated, she has not lost her integrity.
Although love for her was violated, she has not lost her capacity to love.
We affirm her wholeness, her goodness, her truthfulness, her integrity, her ability to love.
We dispel the forces of destruction, and the abuse of power and trust which seek to make her a victim.

Speaking out

(The person/people who have been abused speak, if they wish, about what has happened – maybe from a prepared statement if that is easier.)

Act of liberation

(Candles are lit and, if desired, statements can be burned.)

MINISTER   We light the candle of her spirit. O God, as *N* goes
           down into the depths of her being:
           Show her the hidden things, the creatures of her
           dreams, the storehouse of forgotten memories, hurts,
           strengths.
           Take her to the spring of her life and tell her her
           nature has her name.
           Give her freedom to grow so that she may become
           that self, the seed of which was planted in her at her
           making.

ALL   Out of the depths do we cry to you, O God.

MINISTER   Listen to the language of your wounds, *N*.
           Do not pine away in the pain of your wounds, but
           live from the depths of them, making the extent of
           your desolation the extent of your realm.
           The wounded, frightened child within you needs
           your adult, caring strength, so that the gift she is
           protecting may be yours.
           May our only wounds be these:
           the wound that we cannot avoid because we belong
           to each other,
           and feel and hear the murmur of the world's pain;
           the wound of a sense of compassion for others;
           the wound of a sense of longing for God, the source
           of life and love, deep within us and far beyond us.

The anointing

*(A jug of oil and a small pot may be passed around for each person to
put a drop of oil into. Oil from the pot is used to anoint the survivor and
is symbolic of the affirmation of the group. People may also like to
gather close.)*

(*The lips, hands and feet*)

MINISTER From all violence to your body, be healed.

ALL   Be healed.

(*The breast*)

MINISTER From all violence to your feelings and spirit, be
          healed.

ALL   Be healed.

(*The forehead*)

MINISTER From all violence to your mind, be healed.

ALL   Be healed.

MINISTER The Creator Spirit surrounds you, upholds you on all
          sides, flows round you, caresses you, loves you and
          wills you to be whole.

          N, be whole. Love your body.

          You are a body, not a no-body or just any-body, but
          some-body.

          And we are a body; we are the body of Christ.

          The body is the dwelling place of the whole-making
          Spirit.

          You are a body in the Spirit.

Conclusion

          Be in love with life,
          wrestle with the chaos and the pain,
          with yourself and others,
          spirit echoing Spirit,
          trusting in the victory of the vulnerable,
          glimpsing the peace,
          the wholeness, the spaciousness,
          the justice and the joy
          that comes from following the Pioneer
          made perfect in suffering,

striving and yearning and crying out
from the very depths and heights
of the world's anguish and the world's bliss,
and so becoming friends and partners of God
in divine creating.

A blessing

And the God of peace,
who abhors violence
and gives power to the powerless
fill you with love and grace
and let you go into new life.

The peace
(Shared in the customary manner.)
ALL   The peace of God be with us always.

Material for this service has been taken from a number of sources,
including the following:

Janet Morley, *All Desires Known* (MOW/WIT, 1988)
Jim Cotter, *Prayer at Night* (Cairns Publications, 1991)

Other parts of the service have been adapted from Rosemary
Ruether, *Women-Church* (Harper and Row, 1988).

Teresa Parker is willing to discuss the use of this service: Words
for Worship, Women in Theology, c/o Anne Pounds, 175 Spring
Lane, Hemel Hempstead, Herts HP1 3RD.

Prayers for those suffering from addiction or AIDS

For those suffering from addiction

O blessed Jesus, you ministered to those who came to you. Look with compassion upon all who through addiction have lost their health and freedom. Restore to them the assurance of your unfailing mercy; remove the fears that attack them; strengthen them in the work of their recovery; and to those who care for them, give patient understanding and persevering love, for your mercy's sake.   (10)

And their families and friends

Lord Jesus Christ,
we know the awful consequences of addiction
for in *N* we live with them day by day.
Exhausted beyond patience
we are fearful for his/her future
and our capacity to cope.
In our weakness let us know also your strength
and in your compassionate care find new hope.
This we ask for *N*'s sake and in the power of your name. (19)

For those with AIDS

MINISTER   God calls us as a people in whom no one is expendable. We are called to bear witness to the good news that no one is a stranger or outsider; that in Jesus all division and separation have been broken down. In the face of the world crisis of AIDS, we are called to be one people and yet hardness of heart, discrimination and oppression prevent us from being whom

God calls us to be. For this we seek forgiveness.

God of compassion, we often misrepresent you as a God of wrath, yet you are the God of love, raising us all to life; and so we ask:

ALL Jesus, remember me when you come into your kingdom.

MINISTER Lord Jesus, you banish the fear that has paralysed us, your Church, in responding to the needs of all who are affected by HIV or AIDS. When we falter, encourage us and strengthen us; and so we ask:

ALL Jesus, remember me when you come into your kingdom.

MINISTER Spirit of unity, you build us up when we break down; you gather in when we exclude; you affirm when we condemn; and so we ask:

ALL Jesus, remember me when you come into your kingdom.   (11)

As those who keep the night watch look for dawn,
so, Lord, we look for your help.
May a cure be found;
may we live positively;
may we find love to strengthen us
and free us from fear;
in the name of him who by dying
and rising again conquered death
and is with us now, Jesus Christ.   **Amen.**   (11)

Strengthen our confidence and give us true comfort in the knowledge that, as night follows day and day follows night, God's faithfulness will be with us every moment of our lives. Even if we are unfaithful, God will remain faithful, for God will not deny the very God-self in whose image we have been created.   (11)

A prayer for strength in time of need

> Lord Jesus Christ, you stretched out your arms in love on the hard wood of the cross that all might come within your saving embrace: strengthen all who bear heavy burdens, refresh the weary, cheer the sad, cherish the loveless and grant your peace and joy to all.   **Amen.**   (11)

8

Death and bereavement

At the time of death

Every experience of ministering to a dying person is unique; it is, therefore, neither possible nor desirable to make a single provision to suit all occasions.

There follows a selection of texts from which some choice can be made. It is, however, recommended that first prayer, expressing hope in the living God, should be used.

The longer litanies are supplied with responses; these might be used. However, it may be that a pause after every petition is more suitable. It will usually be appropriate to make a selection from the petitions.

It is most important to allow time for reflection between the various prayers and devotions.

Prayers

In the Name of the Father and of the Son and of the Holy Spirit. **Amen.**

MINISTER Magnified and sanctified be the great Name of God in the world which he created according to his will. May he establish his kingdom in your life and in your days, and in the lifetime of all his people: quickly and speedily may it come; and let us say Amen.

ALL   Blessed be God for ever!

MINISTER   Blessed, praised and glorified, exalted, extolled and
           honoured, magnified and lauded be the Name of the
           Holy One; blessed be God! Though he be high above
           all blessings and hymns, praises and consolations,
           which are uttered in the world; and let us say
           Amen!

ALL   Blessed be God for ever!

MINISTER   May there be abundant peace from heaven and life
           for us and for all people; let us say Amen!

ALL   Blessed be God for ever!   (8)

Short texts

> Who can separate us from the love of Christ?
>
> *Romans 8.35*

> I believe that I shall see the goodness of the Lord in the
> land of the living.
>
> *Psalm 27.13*

> The Lord Jesus says, I go to prepare a place for you, and
> I will come again to take you to myself.
>
> *John 14.2–3*

> Into your hands, Lord, I commend my spirit.
>
> *Psalm 31.5*

(A suitable Psalm may be used.)

Intercessions

> Almighty God, look on this your servant, lying in great
> weakness, and comfort him/her with the promise of life
> everlasting, given in the resurrection of your Son, Jesus

Christ our Lord. (21)

MINISTER God the Father,
Have mercy on your servant.
God the Son,
Have mercy on your servant.
God the Holy Spirit,
Have mercy on your servant.
Holy Trinity, one God,
Have mercy on your servant.
From all evil, from all sin, from all tribulation.

ALL Loving God, deliver him/her.

MINISTER By your holy incarnation, By your cross and passion,
By your precious death and burial,

ALL Loving God, deliver him/her.

MINISTER By your glorious resurrection and ascension, and by
the coming of the Holy Spirit,

ALL Loving God, deliver him/her.

MINISTER We sinners beseech you to hear us, Lord Christ: that
it may please you to deliver the soul of your servant
from the power of evil, and from eternal death.
We beseech you to hear us, loving God.

ALL We beseech you to hear us, loving God.

MINISTER That it may please you to grant him/her a place of
refreshment and everlasting blessedness,

ALL We beseech you to hear us, loving God.

MINISTER That it may please you to give him/her joy and gladness in your kingdom, with your saints in light,

ALL We beseech you to hear us, loving God.

MINISTER Jesus, Lamb of God:

ALL Have mercy on him/her.

MINISTER Jesus, bearer of our sins:

ALL Have mercy on him/her.

MINISTER Jesus, redeemer of the world:

ALL Give him/her your peace. (10)

Let us pray:

God of mercy, into whose hands your Son Jesus Christ commended his spirit at his last hour, into whose same hands we now commend your servant *N*, that death may be for him/her the gate to life and to eternal fellowship with you; this we ask in the name of Christ the Lord.   (13)

Welcome your servant into the place of salvation which because of your mercy, he/she rightly hoped for.

Deliver your servant *N* from every distress.

Deliver your servant as you delivered Noah from the flood.

Deliver your servant as you delivered Rahab and her family from the destruction of Jericho.

Deliver your servant as you delivered Moses from the hand of Pharaoh.

Deliver your servant as you delivered Susannah from her false accusers.

Deliver your servant as you delivered Esther from the plotting of Haman.

Deliver your servant as you delivered the three young men from the fiery furnace.

Deliver your servant as you delivered Daniel from the den of lions.

Deliver your servant as you delivered the adulterous woman from the anger of the crowd.

Deliver your servant as you delivered Jairus's daughter from sickness and death.

Deliver your servant as you delivered Peter and Paul from prison.

Deliver your servant, Lord, through Jesus our Saviour, who suffered death for us and gave us eternal life.   (4)

Prayer of commendation

> Go forth upon your journey from this world, O Christian
> soul, in the name of God the Father almighty who creat-
> ed you: in the name of Jesus Christ, who suffered death
> for you; in the name of the Holy Spirit, who strengthens
> you; in communion with Mary and all the blessed saints
> and aided by the angels and archangels, and all the armies
> of the heavenly host. May your portion be this day in
> peace and your dwelling the heavenly Jerusalem.

> *N*, our companion in faith, the Lord who gave you to us
> is taking you to himself. He who died for you and rose
> again from death, is calling you to enjoy the peace of the
> heavenly city in which there is neither sorrow nor pain,
> and where weakness is transformed into strength. He is
> calling you to see him face to face that you may be made
> like him for ever. He comes to welcome you with angels
> and archangels and all his faithful people that you may
> know in its fullness the fellowship of the Holy Spirit.
> Enter into the joy of your Lord and give glory to him,
> Father, Son and Holy Spirit. (1)

> Into your hands, Lord, our faithful creator and most
> loving redeemer, we commend your child *N*, for he/she
> is yours in death as in life. In your great mercy, fulfil in
> him/her the purpose of your love; gather him/her to
> yourself in gentleness and peace, that, rejoicing in the
> light and refreshment of your presence, he/she may
> enjoy that rest which you have prepared for your faith-
> ful servants; through Jesus Christ our Lord. (1)

Readings
Nunc Dimittis
> Lord now you let your servant go in peace:

your word has been fulfilled.
My own eyes have seen the salvation:
which you have prepared in the sight of every people;
a light to reveal you to the nations:
and the glory of your people Israel.

Luke 2.29–32

Or

I saw a new heaven and a new earth for the first heaven
and the first earth had passed away and the sea was no
more. And I saw the holy city, new Jerusalem, coming
down out of heaven from God, prepared as a bride
adorned for her husband. And I heard a great voice from
the throne saying, 'Behold, my dwelling is with my
people. I will dwell with them and they shall be my
people, and I myself will be with them. I will wipe away
every tear from their eyes, and death shall be no more, for
the former things have passed away.' And the one who sat
upon the throne said, 'Behold, I make all things new.'
Then he said to me, 'It is done! I am the Alpha and the
Omega, the beginning and the end. To the thirsty I will
give water as a gift from the spring of the water of life.'

Revelation 21.1–6

Prayers

Gracious God, nothing in death or life, in the world as it
is or the world as it shall be, nothing in all creation can
separate us from your love. We commend *N* into your
loving care. Enfold him/her in the arms of your mercy.
Bless him/her in his/her dying and in his/her rising again
in you. Bless those whose hearts are filled with sadness,
that they too may know the hope of resurrection in Jesus
Christ our Lord. **Amen.**   (5)

God of love, welcome into your presence your son/daughter N whom you have called from this life. (Release him/her from all his/her sins,) bless him/her with eternal life and peace, raise him/her up to live for ever with all your saints in the glory of the resurrection. We ask this in the name of Christ our Lord. **Amen.** (4)

Loving and merciful God, we entrust our brother/sister to your mercy. You loved him/her greatly in this life: now that he/she is freed from all its cares, give him/her happiness and peace for ever. The old order has passed away: welcome him/her now into paradise where there will be no more sorrow, no more weeping or pain, but only peace and joy with Jesus your Son, and the Holy Spirit for ever and ever. (4)

Lord Jesus Christ, Son of the living God, remember your last hour when on the cross you gave up your spirit to your Father. Set your passion, cross and death between your judgement and us. As we entrust N to you, we pray you to free us from the pains of death and from all wounds of sin, that death may be the gate to life and to unending fellowship with you, for you are the Resurrection and the Life; to you be glory for ever and ever. (1)

N, may Christ give you rest in the land of the living and open for you the gates of paradise; may he receive you as a citizen of the kingdom, and grant you forgiveness of your sins: for you were his friend. (8)

For the family and friends

God of all consolation, in your unending love and mercy for us, you turn the darkness of death into the dawn of new life. Show compassion to your people in their sorrow. Be our refuge and our strength to lift us from the darkness of this grief to the peace and light of your presence. Jesus Christ, by dying for us, conquered death and, by rising again, restored life. May we then go forward eagerly to meet him, and after our life on earth be reunited with our brother/sister where every tear will be wiped away. This we ask through the same Jesus Christ our Lord. **Amen.**

O Lord Jesus Christ, God of all consolation, whose heart was moved to tears at the grave of Lazarus; look with compassion on your children in their loss. Strengthen them with the gift of faith, and give to their troubled hearts and to the hearts of all the light of hope, that they may live as one day to be united again, where tears shall be wiped away, in the kingdom of love; for you died and were raised to life with the Father and the Holy Spirit, God, now and for ever. (1)

Hear the words of the Prophet Jeremiah: 'the sound of mourning and bitter weeping is heard! Rachel mourns her children, refusing to be comforted because her children are no more.'
Like Rachel, we mourn the loss of our loved one. We grieve his/her loss, longing to share with him/her once again.
And Jesus said: 'Blessed are they who mourn, for they shall be comforted.' We seek comfort in our loss. Come Holy Spirit, send your cool breeze to ease the pain of our grieving hearts. (11)

Ending
MINISTER With God there is mercy and fullness of redemption;

let us pray as Jesus taught us:

ALL   Our Father ...

Lord Jesus Christ, our Redeemer. You willingly gave
yourself up to death so that all people might be saved and
pass from death to new life. Listen to our prayers and
look with love on your people who mourn and pray for
their brother/sister *N*. By dying you opened the gates of
life for those who believe in you: do not let our
brother/sister be parted from you, but let your glorious
power give him/her light, joy and peace in Heaven,
where you live for ever and ever.   (4)

May he/she rest in peace.   **Amen.**

After a death

There may be times after a death when, for one reason or another,
members of the family or close friends are unable to attend the
funeral. Below is a short service that might be used.

It will be important to ensure that there is plenty of opportunity for the expression of more personal thoughts.

Opening

In the Name of the Father and of the Son and of the Holy
Spirit. **Amen.**

Collect

O God, the maker and redeemer of all, grant to us, with
your servant *N* and all the faithful departed, the sure ben-
efits of your Son's saving passion and glorious resurrection; that in the last day, when you gather up all things in

Christ, we may with them enjoy the fullness of your promises; through Jesus Christ our Lord, who lives and reigns with you in the unity of the Holy Spirit, God for ever and ever.

Or

God of all, who brought us to birth and in whose arms we die: in our sadness (and shock) contain and comfort us, embrace us with your love, give us hope in our confusion and grace to let go into new life; through Jesus Christ our Lord. (29)

Reading

We believe that Jesus died and rose again; and so it will be for those who died as Christians; God will bring them to life with Jesus. Thus we shall always be with the Lord. Comfort one another with these words.

1 Thessalonians 4.14, 17–18

I am sure that neither death, nor life, nor angels, nor principalities, nor powers, nor things present, nor things to come, nor height, nor depth, nor anything else in all creation, will be able to separate us from the love of God in Christ Jesus our Lord.

Romans 8.38–39

(This might be a suitable point to reflect upon the life of the person who has died.)

Intercessions
(Petitions for the family and friends may be offered, together with other appropriate prayers; at the end:)

Almighty God, before whom live all who die in the Lord:

receive our brother/sister into the courts of your heavenly
dwelling place. Let his/her heart and soul now ring out in
joy to you, the living God of those who live. This we ask
through Jesus Christ our Lord.   (10)

The Lord's Prayer

Let us pray for the coming of the kingdom as Jesus taught
us . . .

Our Father . . .

Now to the one who is able to keep us from falling and set
us in the presence of the divine glory; to the only God our
Saviour be glory and majesty, dominion and power now
and ever. **Amen.**

Before a funeral

At the door

With faith in Jesus Christ, we receive the body of our
brother/sister *N* for burial (*or whatever*). Let us pray with
confidence to God, the Giver of life, that he will raise
him/her to the perfection of the company of saints.   (10)

In the waters of baptism, *N* died with Christ and rose
with him to new life. May he/she now share with him
eternal glory.   (12)

(*Sentences from suitable Psalms may be used. (See page 110.)*)

Greeting
MINISTER The Lord be with you.
ALL   And also with you.

Or

In the Name of the Father, the Son and the Holy Spirit.
Amen.

Collect

Lord God, you are attentive to the voice of our pleading.
Let us find in your Son comfort in our sadness, certainty
in our doubt, and courage to live through this hour. Make
our faith strong through Jesus Christ our Lord.   (3)

O God, the maker and redeemer of all, grant to us, with
your servant *N* and all the faithful departed, the sure ben-
efits of your Son's saving passion and glorious resurrection; that in the last day, when you gather up all things in
Christ, we may with them enjoy the fullness of your
promise; through Jesus Christ our Lord, who lives and
reigns with you in the unity of the Holy Spirit, God for
ever and ever.

Merciful and compassionate God, we bring before you
our grief and loss of *N* and ask for courage to bear it. We
bring you our thanks for all you give us in those we love;
and we bring you our prayers for peace of heart in the
knowledge of your mercy and love, in Christ Jesus our
Lord.   (5)

Deliver your servant, *N*, O Sovereign Lord Christ, from
all evil, and set him/her free from every one; that he/she
may rest with all your saints in the eternal habitations;
where with the Father and the Holy Spirit you live and

reign, one God, for ever and ever.   (10)

(A suitable reading may be used. (See page 119.))

Intercessions

MINISTER Father, we come to you in our grief, trusting in your
          love for *N* and for ourselves. We know that death
          cannot separate us from your love in Jesus Christ our
          Lord.
          This is our faith.
ALL   Lord, increase our faith.
MINISTER Father, your Son Jesus wept at the tomb of Lazarus.
          We believe that you share our grief and will give us
          strength in our loss.
          This is our faith.
ALL   Lord, increase our faith.
MINISTER Father, you gave your only Son, that all who have
          faith in him may not die, but have eternal life.
          This is the faith of the Church.
ALL   This is our faith. **Amen.**   (28)

MINISTER Dear friends: it was our Lord Jesus himself who said,
          'Come to me, all you who labour and are burdened,
          and I will give you rest.' Let us pray, then for our
          brother/sister *N* that he/she may rest from his/her
          labours and enter into the light of God's eternal
          sabbath rest.
          Receive, O Lord, your servant for he/she returns to
          you.
ALL   Into your hands, O Lord, we commend our
          brother/sister *N*.
MINISTER Wash him/her in the holy font of everlasting life, and
          clothe him/her in his/her heavenly wedding garment.
ALL   Into your hands, O Lord, we commend our
          brother/sister *N*.

MINISTER   May he/she hear the words of invitation, 'Come, you
      blessed of My Father.'
ALL   Into your hands, O Lord, we commend our
      brother/sister *N*.
MINISTER   May he/she gaze upon you, Lord, face to face, and
      taste the blessedness of perfect rest.
ALL   Into your hands, O Lord, we commend our
      brother/sister *N*.
MINISTER   May angels surround him/her and saints welcome
      him/her in peace.
ALL   Into your hands, O Lord, we commend our
      brother/sister *N*.
MINISTER   Almighty God, our Father in heaven, before whom
      live all who die in the Lord: receive our brother/sister
      into the courts of your heavenly dwelling place. Let
      his/her heart and soul now ring out in joy to you, O
      Lord, the living God of those who live. This we ask
      through Jesus Christ our Lord.   (10)

The Lord's Prayer

With God there is mercy and fullness of redemption: let
us pray as Jesus taught us . . .

Or

Let us pray for the coming of the kingdom as Jesus taught
us . . .
Our Father . . .

Blessing

MINISTER   Rest eternal grant unto him/her, O Lord.
ALL   And let light perpetual shine upon him/her.
MINISTER   May he/she rest in peace.

ALL   Amen.

MINISTER   May his/her soul and the souls of all the (faithful)
             departed, through the mercy and love of God, rest in
             peace.

ALL   Amen.

MINISTER   May the love of God and the peace of the Lord Jesus
             Christ console you and gently wipe away every tear
             from your eyes; and the blessing . . .   (12)

Prayers for ministry in specific circumstances of death and grief

A baby (see also page 26ff.)

To you, gentle Father, we humbly entrust this child so
precious in your sight. Take him/her into your arms and
welcome him/her into your nearest presence where there
is no sorrow, no weeping, no pain, but the fullness of
peace and joy with you for ever and ever.   (12)

A young person

Eternal God, your wisdom governs the length of our
days. We mourn the loss of *N*, whose life has passed so
quickly, and we entrust him/her to your mercy. Welcome
him/her into your heavenly dwelling and grant him/her
the happiness of everlasting youth. We ask this in the
name of Jesus Christ our saviour and redeemer.   (12)

A sudden death

Unchanging God, as we mourn the sudden death of *N*,
hear our prayers that he/she may know your everlasting

peace. May we know the great power of your love, find
strength in our faith and courage to face this time of trial
in company with Christ our Lord.   **Amen.**

A suicide

God and Father of our Lord Jesus Christ
you are the Father of a crucified
son and know well the anguish of a broken heart.
For *N* the trials of this world are
over and death is past. To your tender
mercy we commend him/her now.
Accept from us all that we feel
when words fail.
Defend us from despair,
hold us in our pain,
and give us strength to meet whatever comes
in the faith of the same Jesus Christ our Lord.   **Amen.**   (19)

God, the lover of souls, you hold dear what you have
made and spare all things for they are yours.
Look gently on *N* who is now beyond
the reach of darkness and despair,
but not beyond the touch of your care and love.

The ending of his/her earthly life seems senseless.
We cannot fathom the anguish of mind he/she went
through.

Forgive us for those times and ways
we failed him/her.
Help us to forgive him/her
for any hurt he/she has inflicted on us:
help us to forgive ourselves
for any harm we fear we may have caused him/her.

Give us grace to release him/her to you,
in the assurance and hope
that you will show him/her the path of life
and lead him/her to walk in your presence
in the land of the living.   **Amen.**   (21)

Violent death

Merciful God,
hear the cries of our grief
for you know the anguish of our hearts.
It is beyond our understanding
and more than we can bear.
Accept our prayer that as *N*
has been released from this world's cruelty
so may he/she be received
into your safe hands
and secure love.
May justice be done
that we may treasure the memory of his/her life
more than the manner of his/her death.
For Christ's sake.   **Amen.**   (17)

Prayer with a child

Please listen God
while we talk to you about *N* who has died.
Take care of him/her and please take care of us too.
Thank you for the times we had together.
Thank you for Jesus who shows us your love.
He is close to *N*, and he is close to us.
Thank you God.   (5)

Anniversary of death

God of time and eternity, we remember *N* who died on this day in years past. As he/she remains in our love, though parted from us, we pray that you will keep him/her in your perfect and infinite care; and that one day we may enjoy friendship with each other in your nearer presence, where every tear shall be wiped away.

9

Life situations

Grace at meals

For this food before us
and the persons beside us
we give you thanks, O Lord.   (19)

May the presence of Christ
bless our table
and the peace of Christ
be the fruit of our sharing.

After meals

Grant O Lord that as we live by your bounty,
we may also live to your glory.

Dedication of gifts

We dedicate this gift
received now with gratitude,
to be held in honour
and respected with care,
in the name of the Father, the Son and the Holy Spirit,
one God who lives and reigns for ever and ever.   (19)

To the Lord our God
who created all things,
by whose will they were created
and have their being,
to him who alone is worthy to receive them,
be glory and honour and power.   (21)

Education

For Christian education

Almighty God, our heavenly Father, you have committed
to your Holy Church the care and nurture of your children. Enlighten with your wisdom those who teach and
those who learn, that, rejoicing together in the knowledge of your truth, we may worship and serve you from
generation to generation, through Jesus Christ our Lord.
Amen.   (26)

For schools and colleges

Almighty God, behold with your gracious favour our
universities, colleges and schools, that knowledge and
wisdom may be increased among us. Bless all who teach
and all who learn, and grant that in humility of heart they
may ever look to you, the source of all truth, through
Jesus Christ our Lord.   **Amen.**   (26)

O God, source of all truth, judge of all people, bless the
labours of those who study, those who teach and those
who add to the store of our knowledge. Show us how to
transform learning into wisdom and technology into service, so that all our study may be dedicated to your glory,
through Jesus Christ our Lord.   **Amen.**   (26)

Work

For a right attitude towards our work

O God, as your Son, Jesus Christ, was obedient to his knowledge of your purposes for him, help us to understand and obey your purposes for us, and to discover the work we are best fitted to do. And as he steadfastly rejected the temptation to use unworthy means, teach us also to accept the discipline necessary to master our work, and to work for the ends that you desire, to the honour of your holy name.   **Amen.**   (26)

For our daily work

Almighty God, you give us new life, new hope and new opportunities with each returning day. Help us to use these blessings to the best of our capacity in doing the work which we have to do, devoting ourselves wholly to your service, and putting our selfish interests aside to seek the welfare of our neighbour, for the sake of him who came among us as one who serves, your Son, Jesus Christ our Lord.   **Amen.**   (26)

For those whose work is difficult

Lord, you have taught us that we are members of one another; hear our prayer for all who do tedious, dirty and dangerous work which is necessary to sustain our life, and grant that all who depend upon their service may remember them with thanks, through Jesus Christ our Lord.   **Amen.**

(26)

For the unemployed

Heavenly Father, we remember before you those who suffer want and anxiety from lack of work. Guide the people of this land so to use their wealth and resources that everyone may find suitable and fulfilling employment and receive just payment for their labour, through Jesus Christ our Lord.   (41)

Journeys

Heavenly Father, protector of all who trust in you,
guide *N* and *N* in their travels today.
As you led your pilgrim people through the desert
and brought them to the promised land,
so protect *N* and *N* from all harm
that they may arrive safely
at their journey's end.   (19)

May our Lord Jesus Christ
be with you to defend you,
within you to keep you,
before you to lead you,
behind you to guard you,
and above you to bless you
now and always.

The Aaronic blessing

N, unto God's gracious mercy and protection I/we
  commit you.
The Lord bless you and keep you.
The Lord make his face to shine upon you,
and be gracious to you.
The Lord lift up the light of his countenance upon you
and give you his peace now and forever.

In court

Reading

> Jesus said: 'When they bring you before the synagogues, and the rulers and authorities, do not be anxious how or what you are to say; for the Holy Spirit will teach you in that very hour what you ought to say.'
>
> *Luke 12.11*

For a witness in court

> Compassionate God and merciful judge hear our prayer for *N* called now to give evidence in court.
>
> By the power of the Holy Spirit enable him/her to speak without fear or favour. Deliver him/her from all anxiety that with unclouded memory he/she may bear witness to the truth with clarity and confidence through Jesus Christ our Lord. (19)

Facing trial

> Merciful God, you do not abandon us in trouble nor ever leave us to our fate. Give *N* patience to endure this time in the confidence that truth will be established and justice be done. Sustain his/her family and friends that supported by their care he/she may be strengthened to meet this trial in the faith of Jesus Christ our Lord. (19)

Anxiety

God with Us

> Father abide
> Christ beside
> Spirit reside
> The Three shield
> From hate
> From harm
> From death's alarm.
>
> Lord be with *N* and *N*;
> In their weakness
> Be their strength
> In their troubles
> Be their peace
> In their danger
> Be their shelter
> In their fears
> Be their hope
> And be with them evermore. (25)

God Between
(*In this prayer the word 'me' could be changed to 'you', or the person's name.*)

> Be the strength of God
> Between me and each weakness
> Be the light of God
> Between me and each darkness
> Be the joy of God
> Between me and each sadness
> Be the calm of God
> Between me and each madness
> Be the life of God

Between me and each death
Be the Spirit of God
Between me and each breath
Be the love of God
Between me and each sigh
Be the Presence of God
With me when I die.   (25)

10

Additional resources

Blessing of water

God our Father, your gift of water brings light and freshness to the earth, it washes away sins and brings eternal life. Bless and hallow this water. Renew the living spring of your life within us, and protect us in spirit and body, that we may be free from sin and serve you in purity of heart: this we ask through Jesus Christ our Lord. (13)

A simple form of Office (16)

What follows is intended for those rare occasions when, at the time when one would wish to say an Office, any more regular provision is quite inaccessible.

Blessed be God, Father, Son and Holy Spirit. **Amen.**

In the morning

Come, let us sing to the Lord:
let us shout for joy to the rock of our salvation.

Let us come before his presence with thanksgiving:
and raise a loud shout to him with psalms.

For the Lord is a great God:
and a great king above all gods.

In his hand are the depths of the earth;
and the heights of the hills are his also.

The sea is his, for he made it:
and his hands have moulded the dry land.

Come, let us bow down and bend the knee:
and kneel before the Lord our Maker.

For he is our God,
  and we are the people of his pasture
  and the sheep of his hand:
O that today you would hearken his voice.

'Harden not your hearts,
  as your forebears did in the wilderness:
at Meribah, and on that day at Massah,
  when they tempted me.

They put me to the test:
though they had seen my works.

Forty years long I detested that generation and said:
"This people are wayward in their hearts;
they do not know my ways."

So I swore in my wrath:
"They shall not enter into my rest." '

In the evening

Behold, now, bless the Lord,
  all you servants of the Lord:
you that stand by night in the house of the Lord.

Lift up your hands in the holy place
 and bless the Lord:
the Lord who made Heaven and earth
 bless you out of Zion.

A psalm
The psalms and canticles are usually followed by:

Glory be to the Father and to the Son and to the Holy
Spirit: as it was in the beginning, is now and shall be for
ever. **Amen.**

Reading

In the morning

Blessed be the Lord, the God of Israel:
for he has come to his people and set them free.

He has raised up for us a mighty Saviour:
born of the house of his servant, David.
Through his holy prophets, he promised of old:
that he would save us from our enemies,
from the hands of all that hate us;

He promised to show mercy to our forebears:
and to remember his holy Covenant.

This was the oath he swore to our father Abraham:
to set us free from the hands of our enemies,

Free to worship him without fear:
holy and righteous in his sight, all the days of our life.

You, my child, shall be called the prophet of the Most
   High:
for you will go before the Lord to prepare his way,

To give his people knowledge of salvation:
by the forgiveness of all their sins.

In the tender compassion of our God:
the dawn from on high shall break upon us,

To shine on those who dwell in darkness
   and the shadow of death:
and to guide our feet into the way of peace.   (42)

In the evening

My soul proclaims the greatness of the Lord:
my spirit rejoices in God my Saviour,

For he has looked with favour on his lowly servant:
from this day all generations will call me blessed.

The Almighty has done great things for me
and holy is his name.

He has mercy on those who fear him;
in every generation.

He has shown the strength of his arm:
He has scattered the proud in their conceit.

He has cast down the mighty from their thrones:
and has lifted up the lowly.

He has filled the hungry with good things:
and the rich he has sent away empty.

He has come to the help of his servant, Israel:
for he has remembered his promise of mercy.

The promise he made to our forebears
to Abraham and his children for ever.   (42)

Intercessions
Our Father . . .

Collects

In the morning

Grant us, O Lord, to pass this day in gladness and in peace, without stumbling and without sin; that reaching evening victorious over all temptation, we may praise you the eternal God, who governs all things world without end.   **Amen.**   (15)

In the evening

Be with us, Lord, for it is evening and the day is far spent; be with us and your whole Church. Be with us in the evening of the day, in the evening of life, in the evening of the world. Be with us and all your faithful people, O Lord, in time and in eternity.   **Amen.**   (15)

A simple form of confession and absolution (40)

MINISTER In the name of the Father, and of the Son, and of the
Holy Spirit. **Amen.**
Jesus said, 'There is more joy in heaven over one sinner who repents than over ninety-nine righteous
people who have no need of repentance.'
This is a saying you can trust:
God in his mercy has saved us
through the washing and rebirth and renewal of the
Holy Spirit,
so that with hope we may enter the life of the
kingdom.

May the Lord be in your heart and on your lips
that you may find the truth that sets us free
and confess your sins with true sorrow.

Confession and counsel

MINISTER Christ is present with us:
he looks on your sorrow and hears your prayer,
Therefore open your heart
and confess your sins with confidence in his mercy.
PENITENT I confess to almighty God,
before the whole company of heaven,
and you my brother/sister
that I have sinned in thought, word and deed,
and in what I have left undone . . .
(*or other suitable words*)
(*Here the penitent confesses particular sins.*)
For these and all other sins which I cannot now
remember,
I pray for God's grace and ask forgiveness.
(*The minister may, with the consent of the penitent, offer words of
comfort and counsel.*)

Reconciliation

(*The minister invites the penitent to express his sorrow and repentance in his own words or the following:*)

PENITENT   I am sorry and ashamed,
and repent of all my sins.
For the sake of your Son Jesus Christ,
   who died for me,
forgive me all that is past;
and lead me out from darkness
to walk in the light of life.   **Amen.**

(*The minister lays hands on, or extends hands over, the penitent and says the absolution. The minister may use one of the following or any other authorized form of absolution:*)

God who is both power and love,
forgive you and free you from your sins,
heal and strengthen you by his Spirit,
and raise you to new life in Christ our Lord.   **Amen.**

Or

Our Lord Jesus Christ
who, in the power of the resurrection,
entrusts the Spirit of reconciliation to his church,
forgives you and frees you from the bonds of sin:
as a sign and witness of his redeeming love,
I absolve you from all your sins,
in the name of the Father, and of the Son, and of the
   Holy Spirit.   **Amen.**

(*Either or both of the following may be said:*)

MINISTER   Merciful God,
We thank you that you have delivered
this your servant from the power of sin
and restored him/her to your peace
in the fellowship of the Church;
strengthen him/her by your Spirit

that he/she may please you
until he/she comes to the fullness of your eternal
kingdom:
through Jesus Christ our Lord.   **Amen.**

(The minister dismisses the penitent using one of the following:)

MINISTER   The Lord has put away your sins.
PENITENT   Thanks be to God.
MINISTER   Go in peace and pray for me a sinner.
Or
MINISTER   The Lord has freed you from your sins.
            Go now in peace and joy,
            to proclaim in the world
            the wonderful works of God.
PENITENT   Amen. Thanks be to God.

(The minister may add:)

Pray for me also, a sinner.

The Lord's Prayer

Our Father, who art in
  heaven,
hallowed be thy name,
thy kingdom come,
thy will be done,
on earth as it is in heaven.
Give us this day our daily
  bread
and forgive us our trespasses
as we forgive those who
  trespass against us.
And lead us not into
  temptation
but deliver us from evil.
For thine is the kingdom,
  the power and the glory,
for ever and ever.   (9)

Our Father in heaven,
hallowed be your name,
your kingdom come,
your will be done,
on earth as in heaven.
Give us today our daily
  bread.
Forgive us our sins
as we forgive those who sin
  against us.
Lead us not into temptation
but deliver us from evil.
For the kingdom, the power,
  and the glory are yours
now and for ever.   (9)

Selection of Psalms

Advent

Psalm 97

> The Lord is king; let the earth rejoice:
> Let the multitude of islands be glad.
>
> Clouds and darkness are round about him:
> righteousness and justice are the foundations of his
>   throne.
>
> For you, Lord, are most high over all the earth:
> You are exalted far above all gods.
>
> The Lord loves those that hate evil:
> the Lord guards the life of the faithful, and delivers
>   them from the hand of the ungodly.
>
> Light dawns for the righteous:
> and joy for the true of heart.
>
> Rejoice in the Lord, you righteous:
> and give thanks to his holy name.

Christmas

Psalm 113

> Praise the Lord, O sing praises you that are his servants:
> O praise the name of the Lord.
>
> Let the name of the Lord be blessed:
> from this time forward and for ever.

From the rising of the sun to its going down:
let the name of the Lord be praised.

The Lord is exalted over all the nations:
and his glory is above the heavens.

Who can be likened to the Lord our God:
in heaven or upon the earth,

who has his dwelling so high:
yet condescends to look on things beneath?

He raises the lowly from the dust:
and lifts the poor from out of the dungheap;

He gives them a place among the princes:
even among the princes of his people.

He causes the barren woman to keep house:
and makes her a joyful mother of children. Praise the
Lord.

Lent

Psalm 51

Have mercy on me, O God, in your enduring goodness:
according to the fullness of your compassion blot out my
offences.

Wash me thoroughly from my wickedness:
and cleanse me from my sin.

For I acknowledge my rebellion:
and my sin is ever before me.

Create in me a clean heart, O God:
and renew a right spirit within me.

Do not cast me out from your presence:
do not take your Holy Spirit from me.

O give me the gladness of your help again:
and support me with a willing spirit.

The sacrifice of God is a broken spirit:
a broken and contrite heart, O God, you will not
    despise.

Psalm 130

Out of the depths have I called to you, O Lord:
Lord, hear my voice.

O let your ears consider well:
the voice of my supplication.

If you, Lord, should note what we do wrong:
who then, O Lord, could stand?

But there is forgiveness with you:
so that you shall be feared.

I wait for the Lord, my soul looks for the Lord:
more than watchmen for the morning, more, I say, than
    watchmen for the morning.

O Israel, trust in the Lord, for with the Lord there is
    mercy:
and with him is ample redemption.

He will redeem Israel:
from the multitude of his sins.

Easter

Psalm 150

> Praise the Lord, O praise God in his sanctuary:
> praise him in the firmament of his power.
>
> Praise him for his mighty acts:
> praise him according to his abundant goodness.
>
> Praise him in the blast of the ram's horn:
> praise him upon the lute and harp.
>
> Praise him with timbrel and dances:
> praise him upon the strings and pipe.
>
> Praise him on the high-sounding cymbals:
> praise him upon the loud cymbals.
>
> Let everything that has breath praise the Lord:
> O praise the Lord!

Pentecost

Psalm 104

> Bless the Lord, O my soul:
> O Lord my God, how great you are.
>
> Clothed with majesty and honour:
> wrapped in light as in a garment.
>
> You make the winds your messengers:
> and flames of fire your ministers.
>
> Lord, how various are your works:
> in wisdom you have made them all, and the earth is full
>   of your creatures.

When you send forth your Spirit they are created:
and you renew the face of the earth.

May the glory of the Lord endure for ever:
may the Lord rejoice in his works.

Others

Psalm 23

The Lord is my Shepherd:
therefore can I lack nothing,

He will make me lie down in green pastures:
and lead me beside still waters.

He will refresh my soul:
and guide me in right pathways for his name's sake.

Though I walk through the valley of the shadow of
death, I will fear no evil:
for you are with me, your rod and staff comfort me.

You spread a table before me in the face of those who
trouble me:
You have anointed my head with oil, and my cup will be
full.

Surely your goodness and loving-kindness will follow
me all the days of my life:
and I shall dwell in the house of the Lord for ever.

Psalm 24

The earth is the Lord's and all that is in it:
the world and all who dwell therein.

For it is he who founded it upon the seas:
and made it firm upon the rivers of the deep.

'Who can ascend the hill of the Lord?
and who can stand in his holy place?'

'Those who have clean hands and a pure heart:
who have not pledged themselves to falsehood, nor
  sworn by what is fraud.

'They shall receive a blessing from the Lord:
and a just reward from the God of their salvation.'

Such a generation of those who seek him:
of those who seek your face, O God of Jacob.

Lift up your heads, O gates; lift them high,
  O everlasting doors:
and the King of glory shall come in.

'Who is this King of glory?'
'The Lord, strong and mighty, the Lord, mighty in
  battle.'

Lift up your heads, O gates; lift them high,
  O everlasting doors:
and the King of glory shall come in.

'Who is he, this King of glory?'
'The Lord of hosts, he is the King of glory.'

Psalm 43

Give judgement for me, O God,
  take up my cause against an ungodly people:
deliver me from deceitful and wicked men.

For you are God my refuge, why have you turned me
  away:

why must I go like a mourner because the enemy
    oppresses me?

O send out your light and your truth and let them lead
    me:
let them guide me to your holy hill and to your
    dwelling.

Then I shall go to the altar of God, to God my joy and
    my delight:
and to the harp I shall sing your praises, O God my
    God.

Why are you so full of heaviness my soul:
and why so unquiet within me?

O put your trust in God:
for I will praise him yet who is my deliverer and my
    God.

Psalm 46

God is our refuge and strength:
a very present help in trouble.

Therefore we will not fear, though the earth be moved:
and though the mountains are shaken in the midst of
    the sea;

though the waters rage and foam:
and though the mountains quake at the rising of the sea.

The Lord of hosts is with us:
the God of Jacob is our stronghold.

'Be still, and know that I am God:
I will be exalted among the nations, I will be exalted
    upon the earth.'

The Lord of hosts is with us:
the God of Jacob is our stronghold.

Psalm 90

Lord, you have been our refuge:
from one generation to another.

Before the mountains were brought forth or the land
    and the earth were born:
from age to age you are God.

You turn us back to the dust and say:
'Go back, O child of earth.'

For a thousand years in your sight are like yesterday
    when it is past:
and like a watch in the night.

You sweep us away like a dream:
we fade away suddenly like the grass.

In the morning it is green and flourishes:
in the evening it is dried and withered.

For we consume away in displeasure:
we are afraid because of your wrathful indignation.

Our iniquities you have set before you:
and our secret sins in the light of your countenance.

When you are angry, all our days are gone:
we bring our years to an end like a sigh.

The span of our life is seventy years, perhaps in strength
    eighty:
yet the sum of them is but labour and sorrow,
    for they pass away quickly and we are gone.

Who regards the power of your wrath?
who rightly fears your indignation?

So, teach us to number our days:
that we may apply our hearts to wisdom.

Return, O Lord; how long will you tarry?
be gracious to your servants.

Satisfy us by your loving-kindness in the morning:
so shall we rejoice and be glad all the days of our life.

Make us glad by the measure of the days that you have
  afflicted us:
and the years in which we have suffered adversity.

Show your servants your works:
and your splendour to their children.

May the graciousness of the Lord our God be upon us:
prosper the work of our hands; prosper our handiwork.

Psalm 121

I lift up my eyes to the hills:
from where is my help to come?

My help comes from the Lord:
the Maker of heaven and earth.

He will not let your foot be moved:
and he who watches over you will not fall asleep.

Behold, he who keeps watch over Israel:
shall neither slumber nor sleep;

The Lord himself watches over you:
the Lord is your shade at your right hand.

So that the sun shall not strike you by day:
nor the moon by night.

The Lord shall preserve you from all evil:
it is he who shall keep you safe.

The Lord shall watch over your going out and your
    coming in:
from this time forth for evermore.

Nunc Dimittis

Now, Lord, you let your servant go in peace:
Your word has been fulfilled.

My own eyes have seen the salvation:
which you have prepared in the sight of every people.

A light to reveal you to the nations:
and the glory of your people Israel.

A selection of Bible readings (NRSV)

1 Chronicles 29.10–13

Then David blessed the Lord in the presence of all the
assembly; David said: 'Blessed are you, O Lord, the God
of our ancestor Israel, forever and ever. Yours, O Lord,
are the greatness, the power, the glory, the victory, and the
majesty; for all that is in the heavens and on the earth is
yours; yours is the kingdom, O Lord, and you are exalted
as head above all. Riches and honour come from you, and
you rule over all. In your hand are power and might; and
it is in your hand to make great and to give strength to all.
And now, our God, we give thanks to you and praise your
glorious name.'

Job 19.23–27

> 'O that my words were written
>   down!
> O that they were inscribed in a
>   book!
> O that with an iron pen and with
>   lead
> they were engraved on a rock
>   forever!
> For I know that my Redeemer
>   lives,
> and that at the last he will
>   stand upon the earth;
> and after my skin has been thus
>   destroyed,
> then in my flesh I shall see
>   God,
> whom I shall see on my side,
>   and my eyes shall behold, and
>   not another.'

Isaiah 40.12, 15–18

> Who has measured the waters in the hollow of his hand
> and marked off the heavens with a span, enclosed the
> dust of the earth in a measure, and weighed the moun-
> tains in scales and the hills in a balance?
>   Even the nations are like a drop from a bucket, and are
> accounted as dust on the scales; see, he takes up the isles
> like fine dust. Lebanon would not provide fuel enough,
> nor are its animals enough for a burnt offering. All the
> nations are as nothing before him; they are accounted by
> him as less than nothing and emptiness. To whom then
> will you liken God, or what likeness compare with him?

Matthew 28.1–7

> After the sabbath, as the first day of the week was dawning, Mary Magdalene and the other Mary went to see the tomb. And suddenly there was a great earthquake; for an angel of the Lord, descending from heaven, came and rolled back the stone and sat on it. His appearance was like lightning, and his clothing white as snow. For fear of him the guards shook and became like dead men. But the angel said to the women, 'Do not be afraid; I know that you are looking for Jesus who was crucified. He is not here; for he has been raised, as he said. Come, see the place where he lay. Then go quickly and tell his disciples, "He has been raised from the dead, and indeed he is going ahead of you to Galilee; there you will see him." '

Matthew 28.16–20

> Now the eleven disciples went to Galilee, to the mountain to which Jesus had directed them. When they saw him, they worshipped him; but some doubted. And Jesus came and said to them, 'All authority in heaven and on earth has been given to me. Go therefore and make disciples of all nations, baptizing them in the name of the Father and of the Son and of the Holy Spirit, and teaching them to obey everything that I have commanded you. And remember, I am with you always, to the end of the age.'

Luke 1.26–31, 35–38a

> In the sixth month the angel Gabriel was sent by God to a town in Galilee called Nazareth, to a virgin engaged to a man whose name was Joseph, of the house of David. The virgin's name was Mary. And he came to her and said, 'Greetings, favoured one! The Lord is with you.'

But she was much perplexed by his words and pondered what sort of greeting this might be. The angel said to her, 'Do not be afraid, Mary for you have found favour with God. And now, you will conceive in your womb and bear a son, and you will name him Jesus.'

The angel said to her, 'The Holy Spirit will come upon you, and the power of the Most High will overshadow you; therefore the child to be born will be holy; he will be called Son of God. And now, your relative Elizabeth in her old age has also conceived a son; and this is the sixth month for her who was said to be barren. For nothing will be impossible with God.'

Then Mary said, 'Here am I, the servant of the Lord; let it be with me according to your word.'

Luke 23.44–47

It was now about noon, and darkness came over the whole land until three in the afternoon, while the sun's light failed; and the curtain of the temple was torn in two. Then Jesus, crying with a loud voice, said, 'Father, into your hands I commend my spirit.' Having said this, he breathed his last. When the centurion saw what had taken place, he praised God and said, 'Certainly this man was innocent.'

John 1.1–14

In the beginning was the Word, and the Word was with God, and the Word was God. He was in the beginning with God. All things came into being through him, and without him not one thing came into being. What has come into being in him was life, and the life was the light of all people. The light shines in the darkness, and the darkness did not overcome it.

There was a man sent from God, whose name was John. He came as a witness to testify to the light, so that all might believe through him. He himself was not the light, but he came to testify to the light. The true light, which enlightens everyone, was coming into the world.

He was in the world, and the world came into being through him; yet the world did not know him. He came to what was his own, and his own people did not accept him. But to all who received him, who believed in his name, he gave power to become children of God, who were born, not of blood or of the will of the flesh or of the will of man, but of God.

And the Word became flesh and lived among us, and we have seen his glory, the glory as of a father's only son, full of grace and truth.

John 14.1–6

'Do not let your hearts be troubled. Believe in God, believe also in me. In my Father's house there are many dwelling places. If it were not so, would I have told you that I go to prepare a place for you? And if I go and prepare a place for you, I will come again and will take you to myself, so that where I am, there you may be also. And you know the way to the place where I am going.' Thomas said to him, 'Lord, we do not know where you are going. How can we know the way?' Jesus said to him, 'I am the way, and the truth, and the life. No one comes to the Father except through me.'

Romans 5.1–5

Therefore, since we are justified by faith, we have peace with God through our Lord Jesus Christ, through whom we have obtained access to this grace in which we stand;

and we boast in our hope of sharing the glory of God. And not only that, but we also boast in our sufferings, knowing that suffering produces character, and character produces hope, and hope does not disappoint us, because God's love has been poured into our hearts through the Holy Spirit that has been given to us.

Romans 8.35–39

Who will separate us from the love of Christ? Will hardship, or distress, or persecution, or famine, or nakedness, or peril, or sword? As it is written,

'For your sake we are being killed all day long;
we are accounted as sheep to be slaughtered.'

No, in all these things we are more than conquerors through him who loved us. For I am convinced that neither death, nor life, nor angels, nor rulers, nor things present, nor things to come, nor powers, nor height, nor depth, nor anything else in all creation, will be able to separate us from the love of God in Christ Jesus our Lord.

1 Corinthians 13.1–13

If I speak in the tongues of mortals and of angels, but do not have love, I am a noisy gong or a clanging cymbal. And if I have prophetic powers, and understand all mysteries and all knowledge, and if I have all faith, so as to remove mountains, but do not have love, I am nothing. If I give away all my possessions, and if I hand over my body so that I may boast, but do not have love, I gain nothing.

Love is patient; love is kind; love is not envious or boastful or arrogant or rude. It does not insist on its own way; it is not irritable or resentful; it does not rejoice in wrongdoing, but rejoices in the truth. It bears all things, believes all things, hopes all things, endures all things.

Love never ends. But as for prophecies, they will come to an end; as for tongues, they will cease; as for knowledge, it will come to an end. For we know only in part, and we prophesy only in part; but when the complete comes, the partial will come to an end. When I was a child, I spoke like a child, I thought like a child, I reasoned like a child; when I became an adult, I put an end to childish ways. For now we see in a mirror, dimly, but then we will see face to face. Now I know only in part; then I will know fully, even as I have been fully known. And now faith, hope, and love abide, these three; and the greatest of these is love.

Revelation 21.1–7

Then I saw a new heaven and a new earth; for the first heaven and the first earth had passed away, and the sea was no more. And I saw the holy city, the new Jerusalem, coming down out of heaven from God, prepared as a bride adorned for her husband. And I heard a loud voice from the throne saying,
'See, the home of God is among mortals.
He will dwell with them as their God;
they will be his people,
and God himself will be with them;
he will wipe every tear from their eyes.
Death will be no more;
mourning and crying and pain will be no more,
for the first things have passed away.'
And the one who was seated on the throne said, 'See, I am making all things new.' Also he said, 'Write this, for these words are trustworthy and true.' Then he said to me, 'It is done! I am the Alpha and the Omega, the beginning and the end. To the thirsty I will give water as a gift from the spring of the water of life. Those who conquer will

inherit these things, and I will be their God and they will
be my children.'

Further readings in the text are:
    Ecclesiastes 3.1–8 (p. 43)
    Jeremiah 1.4–5 (p. 24 or 26)
    Matthew 2.9–11 (p. 23)
    Matthew 11.2–5 (p. 65)
    Matthew 11.25, 27–30 (p. 60 or 65)
    Mark 2.21–22 (p. 44)
    Luke 2.16–20 (p. 22)
    Luke 2.29–32 (Nunc Dimittis) (pp. 81–2)
    Luke 8.43–48 (p. 60)
    1 Thessalonians 4.14, 17–18 (p. 86)
    Revelation 7.17 (p. 24 or 27)

Sources and Acknowledgements

1 *Ministry to the Sick* (CBF, 1983).
2 Church of England Liturgical Commission, amended draft.
3 Based on *The Book of Alternative Services of the Anglican Church of Canada*, copyright © 1985 by the General Synod of the Anglican Church of Canada. Used by permission.
4 *Pastoral Care of the Sick* (Geoffrey Chapman, 1983).
5 *A New Zealand Prayer Book* (Collins, 1989).
6 *Services for Trial Use* (The Church Hymnal Corporation, New York, 1971).
7 *Patterns for Worship* (Church House Publishing, 2nd edn 1995).
8 *Celebrating Common Prayer* (Mowbray, 1994).
9 *The Alternative Service Book 1980* (Oxford: Mowbray).
10 *Book of Common Prayer* (The Church Hymnal Corporation, New York, 1979).
11 *Daring to Speak Love's Name* (Hamish Hamilton, 1992).
12 Adapted from *The Order of Christian Funerals*, © 1989, 1985, International Committee on English in the Liturgy, Inc. All rights reserved.
13 *Prayers for Use at the Alternative Services* (revised edition, Mowbray, 1986).
14 Excerpt from the English translation of *Holy Communion and Worship of the Eucharist outside Mass*, © 1974, International Committee on English in the Liturgy, Inc. All rights reserved.
15 *Oxford Book of Prayer* (OUP, 1985).
16 *Daily Prayer* (General Synod of the Scottish Episcopal Church, 1988).
17 Jeremy Fletcher.

18   Janet Henderson.

19   Stephen Oliver.

20   *Book of Common Prayer* (amended).

21   *Book of Common Order of the Church of Scotland* (St Andrew Press, Edinburgh, 1994).

22   *The Daily Office* (Society of St Francis, 1992).

23   *Deliverance* (SPCK, 1987).

24   *Exorcism, Deliverance and Healing* (Grove Worship Series No. 44; Grove Books, 1976).

25   David Adam, *Tides and Seasons* (SPCK, 1989).

26   *ECUSA: Prayers, Thanksgivings and Litanies* (Church Hymnal Corporation, New York).

27   Mothers' Union, *Anthology of Public Prayers* (adapted).

28   *An Anglican Prayer Book* (Collins, 1989).

29   Janet Morley, *All Desires Known* (Movement for the Ordination of Women, 1988).

30   St Benedict, *Prayers for Sundays*, ed. Michael Counsell (HarperCollins, 1994), by permission of HarperCollins Publishers Limited.

31   Dag Hammarskjöld, *Markings,* translated by Leif Sjoberg and W. H. Auden (Faber and Faber, 1964), by permission of Faber and Faber Ltd.

32   D. McRae-McMahon, *Echoes of Our Journey* (JBCE, Melbourne, 1993).

33   Adapted from Rudolph Nemser in *Daring to Speak Love's Name.*

34   Adapted from Elizabeth Stuart in *Daring to Speak Love's Name.*

35   Adapted from John Gunstone, from *Prayers for Every-Member Ministries* (Highland, 1994).

36   Adapted from William Barclay, *The Plain Man's Book of Prayers* (Collins, 1959), by permission of HarperCollins Publishers Limited.

37   *Book of Occasional Services* (Collins, 1991).

38   Marjorie Allen, Children's Adviser, Diocese of Birmingham.

39   Chaplaincy Department, Queen's Medical Centre, Nottingham.

40   Liturgical Commission, draft Penitential Rite.

41   Adapted from *Book of Common Prayer* (The Church Hymnal Corporation, New York, 1979).

42   English translation by the English Language Liturgical
        Consultation (formerly the International Consultation on
        English Texts).

Material from *Ministry to the Sick, Initiation Services: A Report by the Liturgical Commission* (GS 1152), *Patterns for Worship* and *The Alternative Service Book 1980* is copyright © The Central Board of Finance of the Church of England and is reproduced by permission of the copyright owner.

Every effort has been made to trace owners of the copyright of material in this book. The editors apologize if any omissions or inaccuracies have occurred, and would be grateful to hear of these, so that they may be remedied in any subsequent editions.